TO RING IN SILENCE

First published in 2008 by
The Dedalus Press
13 Moyclare Road
Baldoyle
Dublin 13
Ireland

www.dedaluspress.com

Editor: Pat Boran

ISBN 978 1 904556 87 9 (bound)
ISBN 978 1 904556 88 6 (paper)

Dedalus Press titles are represented in North America
by Syracuse University Press, Inc., 621 Skytop Road,
Suite 110, Syracuse, New York 13244, and in the UK by
Central Books, 99 Wallis Road, London E9 5LN

Printed and bound in the UK by Lightning Source,
6 Precedent Drive, Rooksley, Milton Keynes MK13 8PR, UK.
Typesetting: Beth Romano / Pat Boran.

Cover image: *Empty Stage* by Catriona O'Connor
www.catrionaoconnor.com

The Dedalus Press receives financial assistance from
An Chomhairle Ealaíon / The Arts Council, Ireland

TO RING IN SILENCE

New and Selected Poems

Paddy Bushe

ACKNOWLEDGEMENTS

The author would like to express his thanks to the editors of the various publications in which many of these poems originally appeared. Dánta Gaeilge le caoinchead *Coiscéim*.

For my mother

Contents

vii

viii

II

V

VI

Introduction

⁓

A few years ago, I was one of the judges of the Strokestown poetry competition for poems in English. The three judges read over 2000 anonymous entries—every one of them—and met in conclave. There wasn't much controversy about the winner: a beautifully achieved version of the story of the Chinese drunken suicide poem, 'Li Bai's Last Poem'. When we turned up to the prize-giving some months later, we discovered a number of remarkable things: first the identity of the writer, Paddy Bushe. Second, that astonishingly he was also the winner chosen from the huge entry of poems in the competition for poems in Irish. Third, and worst of all, that the double-winner was the incoming director of the Strokestown Festival. Obviously, if the judging process had been less above-board and anonymous, we would not have let such a thing happen.

But there could not have been a more appropriate double winner. There can't now be a better writer of poems in Irish and English than Paddy Bushe. And as well as writing expert poems in both languages, he uses every contrast and similarity between the capacities and distinctive strengths of poetry in both languages: translation from Irish to English, both of his own poems and of classics of Irish poetry (though of course the reader is often intriguingly left to guess in which direction the translation is going, or the electricity moving), as well as free-standing poems in Irish or in English, often collocated in the text to let the reader decide where the connection is. There is a wonderful poem, in Irish and English, linking Tennyson with Aogán Ó Rathaille; Hopkins, in a series of poems already much admired, is located on Skellig Michael (a locale of the first importance for Bushe); Spenser's imperialist poetics are put into relief by the terrible massacres in his era at Smerwick, Dún an Óir. Michael Hartnett is a crucial presence throughout since it is arguable that Bushe has now assumed his mantle as the leading poet writing in both Irish and English.

But Bushe's poetic reach extends well beyond Irish and English. I have mentioned Li Bai already; Chinese poetry, and Chinese subjects, are central in *To Ring in Silence*. And the connections with other literatures and cultures extend far beyond these. It is a short step to Sorley MacLean, the greatest poet in Scots Gaelic of the twentieth century. All these resonances are established in the first of the book's six sections; they recur in the later sections, centring on Irish mythology in section III or on significant places of refuge and meaning, homing in on Skellig, in section V.

Furthermore, it is not only with places and languages that Bushe engages: the poems also address other arts (music, drama, painting,) and, most importantly, other areas of discussion. Bushe is an important political poet. Many of his admired earlier poems, centring on ecology, are here. And the coverage by now is immensely wider: the main location here is a world at war. Bushe's technique is so sure, his language so precise and formally accomplished, that he can venture with absolute confidence into the public realm. He never needs to raise his voice: his art is like that of the good teacher who commands respect and attention by an unmistakeable, alert intelligence and unfailing interest. This is well illustrated by a poem like 'Arctic Hare' which is the work of a naturalist, poet and concerned citizen of the world. The hare's 'lime-white coat' is observed at the start as he takes cover in his 'mountain hollow': 'Survival's the thing'. Then the poem opens out to conclude:

But since the world is now a hare between packs,
Trembling in every part, listening in terror
To the bugling of the crazed hunters
Among mountains and plains and deserts,

Here is my wish for this hare in a Greenland hollow:
May no wolf nor owl nor eagle come upon you,
May no tooth nor beak nor talon tear you,
And may your white fur never be dappled with blood.

To Ring in Silence is full of such poetic wonders: for example new versions in Irish and English of some of the best-loved classics of the Irish tradition—'Dónal Óg', Seán Ó Duibhir', 'The Prisoner of Clonmel'. The point here is that Bushe can confidently take on the great translators in the Irish lyric tradition, just as he can measure up to the masterpieces of world poetry. But this is, as well as a book of unflagging poetic power, an important book. If it wasn't a slightly dubious or tainted word by now, you might call it global. Its interests are universal, and it views the world with a kind of clear-eyed, spiritual secularity. It comes as a relief after some celebrated, sometimes half-baked Irish books for which spirituality was claimed. Bushe's work is always rooted in the world: a world of great formal and emotional beauty which is under threat. In a poem like 'During the Bombing of Baghdad' the personal and the global are intricately linked. It is a melancholy fact of our times that the fragility which has traditionally been seen as the condition of the private in the face of huge public forces is now a feature of 'the great globe itself'. This book does a magnificent service to Irish literature and the Irish language, by showing them to be anything but parochial. Its humanism reaches out to all times and cultures and places. We should take note. And it is something of a miracle that a work which is so instructive and thought-provoking is at the same time so riveting and enjoyable.

Bernard O'Donoghue

I

The Poet of the Terraces Remembers

Like nomadic herdsmen, I had thought, they would come
And go, in skin robes and broad-brimmed hats,
With daggers at their multicoloured belts.

I had imagined the sound of hooves and bells
Addressing urgencies of cloud and season,
Of distant grasslands and snow on the high passes.

And in summer, I had thought, they would return
At a gallop, whooping for a festival
With rounds of wild dances, and of stories.

But they came, my poems, like farmers
Doggedly each day along the same paths
Between terraces, hoes on their shoulders.

They bent their backs, scraped and groped
For days and months until they harvested
The sweetest grains, berries that held the light.

And they went each night to the herdsmen's fires,
Danced, heard stories, and traded their harvest
For wide-horned cattle, sleek from the grasslands.

Ar Bhruacha Locha Léin

Pé fá deara dhom triall riamh anseo
Mar fhiach iasachta i ndaingeanchoill Rois,
Tá an splendour fós ag sileadh
Ina chaisí ar fhallaí an chaisleáin,
Tá na beannta fós lán seanchais
Agus fós gach eas ag pocléimnigh
Chun glóir a chéile a shárú.
Ach ní chloisim aon trúmpa tráthnóna
Ag baint macalla as na sléibhte.
Cloisim siosarnach duilliúir,
Lapadaíl an locha, mioncheol na néan
Ag fógairt go bhfuil siad bréan bodhraithe
Ag trúmpaí, bídis á séideadh
Go Rathailleach nó go Tennysónach.
A chuislí na héigse, adeir siad,
Gairimid cabhair oraibh. Aogán agus Lord Alfred,
Cuirigí in aithne bhéasach dá chéile iad.
Caithidís uathu trúmpaí ár mbodhraithe,
Tógaidís griangrafanna dá chéile cois locha.

4

On the Shores of Lough Lene

Indifferent to why I ever came to arrive
Like an alien raven at the forest keep of Ross,
The splendour is still falling
In rivulets on the castle walls,
The surrounding summits still resonate with story
And the cascades still tumble over
One another in glorious competition.
But this evening I hear no trumpet
Beating an echo from the mountains.
I hear the leaves murmuring,
The lakeshore lapping, the birds noting
In minor chords that they're bothered
And blasted by trumpets, whether sounded
In Rathaillean or in Tennysonian mode.
With your finger, they implore, *on poetry's pulse,*
Give us a break. Aogán, Lord Alfred,
Introduce them, respectfully, to each other.
Let them throw away their ear-pounding trumpets.
Let them take photographs, of themselves, beside the lake.

Metamorphosis

I might have missed them, so still
The seals lay on the low-tide slabs.
But for the cure of a tail, the slow
Turn of a head, they were living rocks.

Splendidily pedestalled, they had no need
Of the huge theatricalities of light
Beamed from a hidden sun to play
Against massive Atlantic clouds and sea.

So when my binoculars eclipsed
Cliffs, sky and all perspective,
I was absorbed into their salty rankness,
The folds and wrinkles of their grainy hides.

For hours they basked, while I workd
Doggedly in the garden. Afterwards,
The last sod turned, I watched the tide
In a rising swell break over them.

And seeing their hides grow silky with wetness,
I could feel a quickening into fluency
As they slid their heaviness off the rocks,
Undulating themselves easily into waves.

Rehearsing 'Riders to the Sea'

i.m. Tomás Ó Murchadha

It was, you insisted, not until after the everyday
Business of baking bread and sweeping floors
Was given due weight, that the poetry
Could flow. The stitches must be in place

Before the pattern could find itself.
How, except through the ordinary discoveries
Of each day's rehearsal, could we rise it
To the final "we must be satisfied"?

Around your hospital bed, nobody
Knew the words, much less how to say them.
We could only recall our different days
And bless your changed body, strained and urgent

As a ghost galloping to the shore.
Your everydays are over. Rise it now.

John Donne in Beijing

Conceits flew right out the taxi window
Into the blare of traffic, the muggy,
High-pitched, buying-and-selling streets.
My mind, agape, circled and reeled
Like a compass staggering across the globe
Or a drunk repeating and repeating
*Hall of Divine Harmony, Temple of Buddhist Fragrance,
Stone Staircase of Auspicious Clouds.*

Later, in the hotel, while the television
In the background showed Chinese opera,
Drone and whine pitched themselves into sweetness
As we opened and closed ourselves like a fan
And made that little room an everywhere,
Our own small *Palace of Immortality.*

Canal Buddha

Bougainvillea and dozens of anonymous
Creepers trailed towards the water
From every stilted house and balcony,
As our long-tailed, long-nosed boat
Probed the backwaters of Bangkok's canals.
At house after house I photographed
Miniature temples, layered and decorated
With tiny Buddhas and all due ceremony.

Suddenly, as we floated by yet another one,
Draped with yellow scarves and lotus blossoms,
I thought I heard, in a faraway accent,
A blessing, thick-tongued yet familiar:
Kavanagh, serendipitous in a *stupa*,
A canal-bank shrine for the passer-by.

Ómós do Shomhairle MacGill-Eain

Thig crìoch air an t-saoghal ach mairidh ceòl is gaol

Bóithrín a bhí réaltach le nóiníní
A thionlaic sinn go dtí Hallaig,
Á shní féin go héasca
Suas idir faill agus farraige.

Leanamar ar an gcaonach caoin
Loirg crúibe agus coise,
Céim ar chéim sciorrach
Le fia agus le file.

D'aithris an ghaoth sáile
Aníos ó bharr na dtonnta
Bhéarsaí i measc craobhacha
Lán srónaíl agus sondais.

Chuir beann is ailt is creag
Cluas orthu féin le héisteacht
Agus chiúnaigh cliotar na dtaibhsí
I measc coll is beith is caorthainn.

Bhraith neantóg is driseog bíog
I gclocha na bhfothrach fúthu,
Is glór an bhaird ag séideadh
Síol na tine sa luaithreach.

Agus bhain urchar grá macalla
As an aer mórthimpeall Hallaig
Is bhí an aimsir chaite láithreach
In aiséirí an bhaile.

Homage to Sorley MacLean

There comes an end to the world, but none to music, nor love

It was a boreen stellar with daisies
That conveyed us into Hallaig,
Winding its fluent way
Up between sea and crag.

On the kindly moss we followed
The prints of foot and hoof,
Step by slippery step
With a deer, with a poet.

The salty wind recited
From the wavetops below
Verses between the branches,
Nasal and sonorous.

Summit and cliff and crag
Settled themselves to listen,
And the chatter of ghosts softened
Among hazels, rowans, birches.

Nettles and briars felt a stirring
In the ruins their roots encircled,
And bardic utterance wakening
The spark in dormant embers.

Then a bullet of love resounded
In the air surrounding Hallaig,
And the past was presently alive
In the resurrected village.

High Ground

for Somhairle MacGill-Eain at seventy-five

I learn from you that only he who walks
The stony paths and high, dark corries
Of his own most ambiguous hills, can know
With such grace the incense of bog myrtle

Or the prayer mat of moss among hazels.
Only those who have spent time among
The high, stripped places of the heart can heal
With such tenderness the wounded bird of love.

Only the inheritor of the dispossessed
Could celebrate his scattered kindred
Alive again, deep in their misty woods,
Elusive as Deirdre among rowan and birch.

Your cry from your island rampart
Against the submarines nosing around Europe
Carries the pain of the century, the howl
Of shells bursting the brain of history.

And though indeed the deer may never know
The slow trajectory of love's bullet:
See, still, how much there has been said
While holding stubbornly the high ground.

Crossing Waibaidu Bridge

for Zhang Ye

The moon has suspended your poem over the bridge
And sharpened the bite of the wind off the river.

Long convoys of barges, bow nudging stern,
Are buffeting their dogged way against the current.

I do not know what cargoes they carry,
Or how far up the river they will travel.

Nor do I know anything of your burdens,
The distances you have travelled, or will.

But I think you have bowed to the stern buffeting
Of your life's currents, yet still held your buoyancy.

When this bridge first spanned the river in wood,
It demanded a toll from everyone who crossed.

Now that steel has arched itself into its bones,
Waibaidu exacts no price from those who cross over.

And though you must hold fast to the steel in your mind,
May green sap always rise to blossom in your soul.

(The name Waibaidu signifies that no toll need be paid.)

Isolated Being

after Louis le Brocquy

If there are praying hands, they are raised
Still dripping paint from the viscera,
And the ethereal brushstrokes of the head
Descend towards the deep shadow at the thighs.

If there is substance in the central warmth
And lumpiness of those reds and yellows,
It is realised in their constant absorption
Towards the high, translucent white on blue.

Isolated being, companion of my youth,
Veiled envoy between earth and stars,
Discovered again, you teach me still
That nothing is one without the other.

Blithe Newcomers

Just a day or two in Korea, and still
Jetlagged, trying to orientate ourselves,
We take the mountain path, marvelling
At the calligraphy, among strange trees,
Of butterflies, jet-black, as big as wrens.

Suddenly, as we reach the summit
And all the wooded peaks rise and roll
Horizon beyond horizon to the east,
A familiar, wandering voice, reincarnated,
Transliterating perfectly: *kŭ 'ku, kŭ 'ku.*

Petals

for Philip Casey

The waitress puts a vase of grassland flowers
On the table where I'm reading *The Water Star*.
Hesitant, practising English, she asks its name,
Then frowns at my phrasebook's characters.
Shui Xing? ... But, in water, is no star.

As I mime reflection, pointing to huge distances,
Her eyes light with sudden understanding
And she laughs with delight at the image.
I turn again, smiling, to my book.
Two petals shimmer on the open page.

Zhongdian, 6 July 2000

Li Bai's Last Poem

Li Bai, the poet of the Tang dynasty, is said to have drowned
while drunkenly trying to embrace the moon's reflection in water.

I

The more my boat rocks, the more
Exuberantly the moon disports itself
Among the ripples. I dip my oars

Into one shining facet or another
Of that reflected light, and I zig
And zag somehow to the lake's centre

And spin myself to a shaky stop.
On the shore, a lantern flickers.
I can hear the cry of my peacock

Bounce itself from star to brittle star
And rattle into silence. I uncork
My wine-jug and ceremoniously pour

A measure for myself and a measure
Ceremoniously, as always, for another.

II

All of my life has been other, is absence:
Farewells in wine-shops, Meng Haoran's sail
Diminishing down the length of the Yangtse,

Poems to and from Du Fu, their characters
Like heads bowed in exile, like wild geese
Crossing a cold moon above bare branches.

17

All of those merchants' wives, those distant
Administrators yearning for their families,
Were versions of myself, listening

Desperately for footsteps along the path,
Searching the Milky Way for friends,
Combing the wind for the hermit's flute,

Raising a wine-cup, a jolly good fellow,
Cavorting with the moon and my own shadow.

III

Another cup of wine. The shadowed
Mountains across the lake are watching
Like judges in their long dark robes.

Lighten yourselves! I do not threaten
The order of the state. Let the record show
That even Li Bai was once tempted

By imperial affairs: a court academy,
No less, of compliant poets, commissioned
To spin line after silken line of flattery,

While an emperor searched for immortality
In elixirs, or the arms of Yang Guifei. I sang
His or her praise. For a time, it trapped me.

Listen, moon! That fool of a man, his concubine,
Are less to me here, now, than this cup of wine.

IV

Place, too, becomes a kind of absence
For the wanderer. Even after sixty years
I can still pine for the distant grasslands

Of my childhood, their huge perspectives
Along flowered valleys to the high passes,
The tents, the cattle-bells, the whooping herdsmen.

My breath still catches on the pine-incensed road
Into Sichuan. I sigh day after day for fishermen
Poling bamboo rafts on the river at Yangshuo,

And my heart still scales the hundred terraces
Of Dragon Back Mountain, where white cranes
Walk in a dream, entranced by their own elegance.

Agh, more wine! The traveller's curse
Is to ache to be everywhere, all at once.

V

No more wine. I fling the empty jug
Through space at the moon's reflection
With the rage of a lover whose love

Has turned bitter. The image breaks
Into a thousand slivers that pierce
My eyes, my heart, then turn to flay

Me alive. Alive? There are ways to be alive:
In peach blossoms in spring, in the flow
And flood of the Yangtse, in those high

Stripped places where I must journey soon,
Never again to raise a parting wine-cup.
In the lake's mirror, the shining moon,

That just now I shattered, is shaking
Itself whole again. I must embrace it.

A Present from Newcastlewest

for Angela Liston

This was Michael's favourite stone, you said,
As you opened your fist and closed mine
Around your gift. Instinctively I paused, anticipating
The pun, the punchline, the Hartnett *coup de grace.*

But there was no joke, just the smooth
Flatness of the finger-polished stone, basalt
I think, its blackness broken by just one
Grey pockmark, beady as a wren's eye

Staring up at me. And the wink I swore
I saw was pure imagination. From our mantelpiece,
You explained. Now it sits on the window-ledge
Above my desk, absorbing the Atlantic,

As I absorb its darkness, its blankness,
Its molten memories, its cooling and settling,
The sea breaking over its shattered columns,
And, in certain lights, its flashes of grace.

Final Version

i.m. Michael Hartnett

Too early. Yes, all of that. But now you've said
A farewell to all language, and are translated
To a version where, definitively yourself,
Sharing elements with hares and otters,
And raising pewter mugs with spailpín poets,
You can hear the pulse-music you knew well
Lies beyond all poems, and before them,
And you cannot be lost in the translation.

Poets at Smerwick

In November 1580 an expeditionary force of 600 Italian and Spanish soldiers landed at Smerwick, County Kerry, to aid the Irish Geraldine rebellion against Queen Elizabeth. They fortified the site of an older fort called Dún an Óir, or Fort del Oro. The fort was besieged and captured by English troops under Lord Grey. On his orders, the expeditionary force was massacred, and their bodies thrown over the cliffs. Some Irish solders and camp followers were tortured and hanged. Elizabeth commended Grey for his actions, regretting only that he had spared some officers.

POSITIONS

> *Then put I certyn bandes who straight fell to execution.*
> *There were 600 slayne.*
> —*Lord Grey's report to Elizabeth*

This is the bare statement.
Details lingering in other gleanings.
How the weapons were dented
From the excess of hacking.
How at the forge, two men,
Bones hammered on an anvil,
Died for three days. Such details
In flat prose can be swallowed
Until the prose throws up two names
That had before been castled gracefully
Among the trees of the Blackwater,
Silver poets of a golden age: Ralegh
Snug in anthologies, Spenser ingenuously
Singing the praises of his Faerie Queene.
But at Smerwick, Edmund Spenser, secretary,
Scripted beautifully Lord Grey's report,
And Walter Ralegh, captain, organised the kill.

ECHOES

Smerwick. A hard Norse ring to it.
Fire and ice beat out the shape.
Raiders with reddened eyes and salt lips
Named it, leaving echoes
Among cliffs like sharp, arbitrary edges.
These heights, those angular consonants,
Echo no woods, frame no soft vowels. Here
Is no Blackwater Valley. Here the bones lie out.

SONNET

The prisoners were penned inside the fort,
An open challenge to Elizabeth.
So Grey, as Spenser wrote in his report,
Thought her best served by their exemplary death.

Thus Walter Ralegh, captain, part-time poet,
Was drafted in to organise the work.
To pike six hundred men was heavy going,
But Ralegh thought it out like any clerk

Compiling figures. Every man must kill
His share. In order that there'd be no doubt,
He'd have to show the carcasses to fill
The quota Walter Ralegh figured out.

The body count worked out at five per man.
That tidy mind would make a sonnet scan.

THE LIE

When Ralegh came out of Ireland,
Did poetry also demand a cloak
To spread over those bloodier pools
He had waded to this more courtly siege
Of his impregnable, capricious queen?
Did any simile leer from the caked
Whiteness of Elizabeth's face,
Or the red gash of her mouth?
Was there, in the surges of the dance,
In those energetic sweating lines,
A sudden dizziness that transformed
The expert forking of sweetmeats
Into the apt, the vital image?
Or did his poet's mind retreat
Into itself, and give him both,
Butterfly and butcher, the lie?

FOOLS' GOLD

Dún and Óir, Fort del Oro.
Named for gold that wasn't there.
Strange how Ralegh blundered
Towards the scaffold, a lifetime later,
Sailing up the Orinoco for gold, no gold,
For El Dorado. Fort del Oro.
Dún an Óir. Beginning
Towards an end. Blood and gold
Like the slashed crimson trunks
Of a courtier dancing in
And out of favour.

Of Gentilnesse

How in its servise, it seemeth necessarie to forget what it did whilom signifie, so that it perish not despite iteselfe. How this enforceth him who serveth politie to consider all things in a double fashione.

Of the Breaking Wave

How it changeth by th'effecte of all the brokene bodies, from being as newe milke to a sauvage redde, as if there hath bene a butcherie of the greate Leviathan.

Of Courtesie

How it changeth constantlie its dresses, from the soldieres stained cloake to the silke of the Courte.

Of Fortune

How, as men doe say, it resembleth a greate wheele which can bringe men up and down by turne. How chieflie, however, it doth breake them as doth the racke.

Of Visionne

How it can be in the same houre the blindnesse of poesie and a view towards advauncement.

QUESTION

A question, Edmund Spenser:
What's the difference between an allegory
And a massacre? Between
A gentil knight was pricking on the plaine
And the grating of a pile against a pelvis?

Between a marriage hymn on the Thames
And pregnant women hanged at Smerwick?
Between your knight's iambic horror at
A dunghill of dead carkases he spide
And the copperplate account you sealed and signed?

AN APOLOGY FOR POETRY

At Smerwick, I watch the gannets
Circle over the unseen shoal,
Staring down the long clarity.

Sunflashes on their white wings
Dazzle. I barely see the black tips
Flick them on course, as they twist

On the instant
(Of scales' panic, too late!)
Of silver sacrifice.

Watching from the cliffs, I see
Necessary angels. I admire
The ordained patterns, their grace.

This is an apology for poetry.

An Mhuintir agus An Éigse

do Ba Da Chai

De thaisme, más ann in aon chor dá leithéid,
A bhuaileamar le chéile, mise ar shiúlóid maidne,
Tusa ag dúnadh dorais. *This my study house.*
What do you study? Make poems. So do I!
Agus away linn díreach go dtí an scoil filíochta agat
(*Peoples and Poems* a d'aistrís an t-ainm le scairt)
Ar bhruach an chuain. Seomra geal, fairsing,
Boird agus mataí ina n-áiteanna féin,
Agus druma mór chun rithime ar an urlár

B'fhada fada sinn ó sheomraí dorcha
Agus clocha ar bhrollach gach ábhar file.
Gach aon fhuinneog níos niamhraí ná a chéile:
Sliogiascairí i gcrithloinnir an lagtrá,
Nóra na bPortach agus éirí-níos-airde uirthi
Leis an gclúmh geal bán a fuair sí anseo timpeall,
Agus Ilch'ubong, Mullach Éirí na Gréine,
Ag taibhreamh ar thine a spalpadh amach arís
Ach an lá a bheith róbhrothallach.

Mhalairtíomar leabhair go deasghnáthúil
Agus d'ólamar té glas go deasghnáthúil,
(Agus ba dheas, gnáthúil mar a dheineamar)
Inár suí go ciarógach ag bord íseal,
Ag tabhairt aitheantas cuí dá chéile.
Agus cé gur bhrathas ar dtús iartharach, tuathalach,
Fiú corrthónach, d'éiríos diaidh ar ndiaidh
Suaimhneach, oirthearach, (Searcenstockach, dá ndéarfainn é)
In Songsan, i dtigh geal sin na filíochta.

Peoples and Poems

for Ba Da Chai

It was by chance, if there is any such thing,
That we met, me out for a morning walk,
You closing a front door. *This my study house.*
What do you study? Make poems. So do I!
And away with us to your school of poetry
(*Peoples and Poems*, you translated the name, laughing)
On the edge of the sea. A lucent, airy room,
Tables and floor-mats, each in its own space,
And a skin drum invoking rhythm on the floor.

We were miles and miles from darkened rooms
And bardic apprentices with stones on their chests.
Each window framed more magic than the next:
Shellfish-gatherers in the shimmering ebb-tide,
Nora the Heron getting even more stuck-up
With the white crane's outfit she picked up around here,
And Ilch'ubong, the Summit of the Rising Sun,
Dreaming about erupting one more time,
Only that the day was far too warm.

We exchanged books politely
And drank green tea, again politely,
(And the ceremony was marvellously everyday)
As we sat cross-legged at a low table,
Eyeing each other with due recognition,
And although I was awkward and western,
You could even say tight-arsed, I became inch by inch
Easier, more oriental, (dare I say Searcenstockian?)
In Songsan, in that luminous house of poetry.

Wine Cup

At Kyonju, beside the tiny stream
Shaped by cut granite to the outline
Of an abalone-shell, I conjure once again
A ceremonial of poets and calligraphers.

From the pavilion I conjure lacquered tables,
Ink-sticks of soot pressed with camphor,
Porcelain brush-pots, silk and layered paper.
Squirrels and moths are flitting in attendance.

I conjure the most venerable among us
To place a brimming wine-cup,
Glazed by candles and moonlight,
Into the exact centre of the stream.

Whenever it grounds itself against the bank,
Like a line that has faltered, the nearest one
Must drink it and compose there and then
Words for the company, characters for the page,

Then fill and float it away again. I wait
As it circles around and around the rim
Of the shell, nodding graciously each time
It passes me, away beyond my conjuring.

Hopkins on Skellig Michael

LANDING

By Christ then but Skellig will test that poor man!
The boatmen dug their oars deep in the swell
And pulled the bow around. *Upon my soul*
He'll know his prayers well after a night
Up there on the cliffs with the screeching birds.
It's a different man we'll be collecting then!
They waved towards the diminishing black figure
Who had knelt to pray on the small pier.
Just like a stranded cormorant, they chuckled,
And bent their back to the oars.
                                    On the pier,
Father Gerard Hopkins had begun his retreat
At the very edge of Europe. *But from what*
Am I retreating? Why do I compound
My exile here in the most extreme corner
Of this most extreme land? England, Ireland,
Have disappeared with that boat and I am here,
Deeper and farther into exile, into isolation.
He remembered the boatmen telling a boy
To carry *the minister's bags,* their disbelief
That his collar was Catholic, the muttered aside
About *a fierce Protestant accent for a priest.*
Head bowed, he endured again the everyday
Claws of exile, the scratches of no harm meant.

STEPS

Steps.
     Stone steps.
          Steps
Cut into stone.
         Step
After stone step.
         Steps
Of stone slab.
        Slab
After worn stone slab.
Edge of stone.
        Step
The edges of stone.
        Step
The edges of soul.
         My soul
Is stone, is splintered slate.
O let my slow
      Plodding
         Hone me,
Edge me with brightness.

SADDLE

Christ's Saddle, he remembered, is the dip
Between the island's two peaks, just before
The final ascent. *You can rest there, Father,*
And gather yourself to go to the top.
Breath seared and legs ached as he sank
Into the sea-campion. Rabbits scattered
Into myriad burrows at the intrusion

And gulls sheered away in raucous protest.
The wind and the querulous birds seemed
To play one and the same note of mockery.
Christ's Saddle. He started at the sudden
Reverberation of the name among the rocks,
Remembering how once in Wales a bird
Had ridden the wind like Christ in glory
While fire broke, lovely and dangerous.
He closed his senses, became a darkness
That curled interminably around itself,
Squeezed brain, body and soul to all or nothing,
Then howled its wounded self deep into the wind.

FINAL FLIGHT

The whole island rose to form a buttress
For the last, exposed steps to the monastery.
Flight, he thought, was the wrong word,
Too easy for these hard-hewn stairs that seemed
To lead to nowhere but their own sheer
Infinity, winding through vertical
Planes where the eye was constantly drawn up
Or dizzily down. The horizons of everyday
Vanished between firmament and abyss.
His mind lurched too, hung once again
Above unfathomed falls, sheer and frightful.

Endure, he whispered, *I will yet endure.*
And crept on hands and knees towards the comfort
Of the high stone cells, out of the wind.

ENCLOSURE

And then to follow the path, level at last,
Across a narrow ledge and to enter
Under huge lintels, the enclosure! A small
Miracle of terracing, and the stone cells
Shaped like beehives, like bells, and all
The air was honey, was chimes, was harmony.
To fall on his knees by the high cross
Where the east to west pitch of the oratory
Encompassed the whole world, while gannets
Circled widely above silvering seas
And all the spheres meshed, was to rise
With the grace of a bird and to wheel
In the infinite circles of God's mind.

SOURCE

They're never dry, those miraculous wells
Right in the heart of the monastery,
He had been told. They sprang into vision,
Full of brackish water. He willed belief,
But curiosity welled stronger in him,
Who had probed the inscape of bluebells,
Patterned a lunar halo, and diaried
Canal water's passage through a lock.
Investigation quickly undermined the miraculous,
Undammed the secrets of the underground
Conduits from the slabs behind the cells,
Grooved and guided into the stone basins.
A miracle still, he mused, *of intent,*
Of will to stay, of work, to channel
Water through stone as grace through spirit.
Laborare orare est. Aqua vita est.

34

STORM

Squall after squall from the black north-west,
Layer upon layer of darkness, stratum
Down stratum of stone-faced time, all
Without rhyme or reason pounded him,
Beat him level in the blurred vastness
Of the storm. The monastery terrace
Was tilting like a panicking deck,
The island was riven stone, splintering
On the shipwreck of itself, itself
Its own cause and cacophonous effect,
Foundering deeper into its own void.
Rain- and spray-blinded, he stumbled to the high
Cross, clung to it, swallowed salt,
Conjured witness, summoned arbitration
Against blankness.
                                    The lighthouse beam flickered
Behind walls of rain, beat against clouds.
Light beat then, too, in his brain, spread
The length of passages smeared with despair,
And sprang in salty relief to his eyes.
Enough, he prayed. *Let me elect to follow,*
And light, though it comes and goes, will shine.
Will the clarion, and the clarion will sound.
And this bare brute, air-brushed, wind-weary and wounded,
Floundered towards light once whole, whole once again.

ETYMOLOGY

Praying, trying to transform morning
Into matins, he was shaken by the screech
Of a peregrine falcon, as a burst puffin

Scattered over the path his office took.
He laid aside the missal, looked for paradigms.

He could see a derivation in the abrupt
Latin, *falx: sickle,* realising those talons
That sliced down layers of brightness
In that appalling plunge, those bloody feathers.
But what consoling pattern could he find
In the *haecceitas* of curved beak tearing flesh
Here, now, on this fanged Atlantic rock?

None, none, in the sickle alone,
Shining or bloodstained, meaningless,
A surd.

Search then, for meaning among other elements.

Peregrine. Wanderer. Per agria.
Wanderer across lands. Peregrinus.
In Roman law, stateless. A stranger.
Wingbeats about his head, clawings at his brain.
Peregrinus. Peregrinatio. Pro Christo.
Peregrinatio pro Christo. Exile.
Pilgrim. Pilgrimage for Christ. For Christ
A stranger, removed, becomes pilgrim,
Becomes hawk like Christ, like Christ a victim,
Is hawk and victim and in Christ's sacrifice
Is one with the world won all at once back.

And he prayed that his ultimate fall might be cushioned
By the hawk sacrificed, in the plumage of Christ.

EMPIRES

Among the stone cells, he considered Empire,
Its porticoes and columns, its bronze statues
In sunlit squares dispensing jurisprudence
Flanked by cannon, the dust of savagery
Settling under the weight of Latin words,
And found it good. He yearned for Latin prayers
To be its yeast, to quicken power into praise
Of the One, Holy Catholic and Apostolic.
He craved the centres, mourned for himself,
Stranded, swept from chronicles and courts
Among people who broke bread with him only
By divine accident, a confusion of history.

The noon sun burnt mist away, settled wind,
Drew heat from bare stone. He found a niche,
And, almost comfortable eased himself into it.
The sun and night's exhaustion closed his eyes.
Margins and centres merged, half-dreamt, on the peak.
Rome and London spun a globe between them.
Imperium! Imperium! boomed the sun,
As its light dissolved, shimmering, in the sea.

LEAVING

By God, he doesn't look too bad. Bobbbing
In the shadow of the rock they hauled
Fish after shining fish aboard. They watched
As he descended slowly from the summit
And heard him call out something to them.
He can wait awhile now. There's a shoal here!
They laughed, spilling out more mackerel.

At last, tired, they pulled ashore, half-expecting
Recrimination, protests of neglect.
But at the pier he waved, and smiled
As they spun the boat showily alongside.
He settled easily on a scaly thwart
And eyed the quivering, thumping fish.
An appropriately miraculous catch, gentlemen,
He offered buoyantly. They smiled politely,
Sensing a joke they did not understand.

There wasn't much talk as they rowed home.
They established he hadn't been too lonely
Or frightened, and all agreed they were blessed
With the calm day after such a bad night.

Anchors

for Mary Golden

In Tripoli, the school cats bask in the shade
Of an olive tree outside the window.
I talk to a class of dark, deep eyes
Fixed on their exams and on Heaney's

The annals say ... and I almost drown
In their strangeness and the day's heat,
So that *Clonmacnoise* and *oratory* grow remote
In space as well as time (stranger even

Than ships that sail freely across the sky)
Until all at once my mind anchors itself
On the upturned boat of Gallarus, marvellous
On a soft day, as I have known it.

At Cúirt in Galway

for Seamus Heaney

The tide race is crazy today, passing itself out
In a mad rush between river and sea,
Running rings around streets and traffic,
Revving over weirs, flat out under bridges.

Where it calms, below the Spanish Arch,
A whole billowing armada of swans is still
Holding the line magnificently against the flow,
Their dogged, webbed effort a measure of grace.

The sun is orchestrating jigs and reels of light
(Around the harbour and mind the jetties),
And mooring chains are clanking out the time
For tipsy masts that nod, a beat or two behind.

And last night's reading lifted up our hearts,
And blew them open, and coaxed them out to dance.
And we're still high. Even mighty. We hoist sail,
Raring to circumnavigate the round of our day.

April 1999

Embracing Yevtushenko

for Joanna Keane

Outside The Listowel Arms,
As farewells played to full houses,
Yevtushenko's long, fluent arms
Circled you and the Writers' Week
You inherited. Then showman
Became shaman so that those long
Fluent vowels conjured
Gilt domes out of slate roofs,
Steppes from the Stacks Mountains
And Vladivostok out of Abbeydorney;
Conjured also a familiar spirit
Who circled The Square, sidled over
From the Kremlin of St. John's
And wondered what the Russian
For *ciaróg* was, for he'd know
His own wordcrafty sort anywhere
In any language, and what
Was the Russian for *plámás?*
And please unhand his daughter
So he could embrace, if we didn't mind,
The apple of his eye for himself.
Laughter boomed and pealed
Like bells around The Square
And while Yevtushenko's long frame
Was poured, still *plámásing,* into a taxi,
Himself slipped away, satisfied.

Kind for you, *créatúr,* to be embraced
By giants, circled by shamans.

Memorial

for Mick and Judy Delap

In Southwark Cathedral, the organ reverberates
Around arch and pillar, urgent with rehearsal.

Its essays in contemporary dissonance scale
The same heights as do its older measures.

Here stone trembles, beating out time
Among slabs inscribed with passing fame.

Beside the south wall, under a burst
Of stained glass teeming with his people,

You find Shakespeare, languid in effigy,
Bland as a grandsire cut in alabaster.

And it's almost a ho and a hey nonny nonny
Until your dutiful eye travels

Down his scalloped sleeve to a hand punkily
Pierced, sporting no rings but, spiky

With renewal, a sprig of greygreen fragrance,
Clutched tight. Here's rosemary, for remembrance.

Afternoon in Kunming

In Green Lake Park, the afternoon crowd
Gathering in and around the pavilion

Was mostly pensioners, old comrades in cards,
Settling companionably near the music.

When the younger woman was called,
She spat to clear her throat before pitching

Her voice so perfectly to the bamboo flute
That applause almost drowned her singing.

And when she danced whatever story
Flowed between the *erhu* and the bells,

Her rayon blouse and fat, miniskirted legs
Liquified themselves into the music,

As cranes might pick their white, reflected way
Dreamily through the mud of patterned terrraces.

I saw the lined, watching faces lift up and shine
Like dry bamboo absorbing morning sun.

Morning on the Night Train

Dawn. The train coughs and splutters,
Taking water at a small, empty station

In the gorge that snakes its dry way
Through the crumbling plateau of Gansu.

Light seeps down the cliffs, gilds
The corrugated iron of the sheds.

When I slide open a window, releasing
Smoke and food smells into the thin air,

Birdsong, something like a thrush,
Overflowing with rise and ripple,

Begins to sprinkle itself on the morning.
A window slides in the next carriage

And eager lips and tongue and throat
Whistle out a stream of perfect mimicry.

I'd swear those bubbling voices join
To pitch themselves up to the still

Wide-eyed stars, charming them
One by one into a dreamless sleep.

Music Lesson, Xiahe

I remember it still, the young monk's delight
At the chance meeting with us on the hill,
The phrase-book hauled from the depths of his robe

Redolent of drawing-rooms and radiantly
Enthusiastic about self-improvement.
He opened it at random, and between

Introductions and *The Rules of Tennis*,
It offered, in English, Tibetan and Chinese,
The vocabulary of *Playing the Piano*.

You both pulled out imaginary stools
And, exquisitely occidental, he read
Would you be so kind as to turn the pages?

He tinkled and jangled the strange consonants
Around his tongue, applauding the right notes,
While *arpeggios* of giggles accompanied mistakes.

And as he fingered the unfamiliar keys
The *basso profundo* of the huge monastery trumpets
Reverberated up the hill, and the great gong

On the roof-top brazenly imposed a silence
That would become the world's one note
In the fragrant, chanting halls below.

And to his *Do you find the music pleasant?*
The phrase-book prompted you: *Simply delightful!*
And it was. And it echoes. Still.

An Veidhleadóir

do Mhartin Hayes

Tá an folt aige ag sileadh ar an veidhlín,
Chomh casta le súgán, chomh catach
Leis an gceol a tharraingíonn sé as.
Is fada an tarraingt é, pé acu a mbíonn

Púcaí ag portaireacht in uaigneas oileáin,
Ríleanna ag ríleáil de shíor ó athair go mac,
Nó sleamhnáin ag sleamhnú thart timpeall a' tí
Agus isteach is amach arís faoi dhó.

Anois lena shúile dúnta is a bhéal ar leathadh
Amhail duine le Dia, tá an téad is téadmhaire
Á tharraingt féin nóta ar nóta go dtí an bhuaic—
Phointe is gaire do Neamh ar feadh soicind

Nó dhó agus anois siúd leis arís go h-obann
Ag aibséileáil síos easanna *arpeggio*
Go dtí an talamh réidh arís. Le teann faoisimh
A bheith thíos, pléascann ár mbosa ag bualadh.

The Fiddler

for Martin Hayes

His mop of hair flows onto the fiddle,
As twisted as a súgán, as curling
As the music he draws from it.
It's a long draw, whether it be

Fairy music echoing an island loneliness,
Reels constantly reeling from father to son,
Or slides that slide the round of the house,
Then advance and retreat again.

Now with his eyes shut and mouth open
Like God's own clown, the supplest string
Is drawing itself note by note to the topmost
Point nearest to Heaven for a second

Or two and suddenly he's off again
Abseiling down waterfalls of *arpeggios*
To level ground again. With the height of relief
At being down, our hands explode into applause.

Cloisfead ar Neamh

Über Sternen muß er wohnen
—Schiller

Bhí Beethoven ar an steiréo, an tigh
Tonnchreathach, líonreathach, gairdeach,
Agus mé ar tí dul ag bothántaíocht
Go dtí mo chomharsa. Níor mhúchas an ceol
Agus d'fhágas dóirse agus fuinneoga ar leathadh
Nuair a shiúlas amach faoi ghile oíche sheaca.
Gotha an stiúrthóra orm, bheannaíos
Go mórchúiseach le ceolfhoireann na réalt,
Sheolas an uile nóta chucu, agus shiúlas liom
Ag súil gur chualathas an ceol ar neamh.

I Shall Hear in Heaven

Über Sternen muß er wohnen
—Schiller

I had Beethoven on the stereo, the house
Wave-shaking, full-flowing, celebrating,
Me gathering myself to go rambling
To my neighbour. I left the music playing,
And the doors and windows wide open
When I walked out into the frosty starlight.
Throwing shapes like a conductor, I bowed
Ceremoniously to the orchestra of the stars,
Signalled every last note to them, and went my way
Hoping that the music would be heard in Heaven.

An Idle Song

for Ishbel MacAskill

Òran dìomhain, an idle song
They'd call it, if it strayed at all

From its long, ordained lines into byways
Of love, of longing, or even of loss.

And if the Devil can indeed make work
For idle hands, then—Heaven knows,

With the way things are today—
What might he do with an idle song?

He might even dare to make a noble call
On the Almighty, and ask God to sing.

And She would, I swear She would, Her sweetness
Astonishing choirs of angels into silence.

> *Air a' bhàd aiseag ann an Caol Ìle,*
> *19/08/2006*

Equinox Concert

for Mícheál Ó Súilleabháin and Mel Mercier

Light and darkness are in balance
All over the globe tonight, the world
Shrinking into itself like a nut
Hardening in its winter shell.

Years turn, and millennia, and ten
Days after the towers burned,
The spheres are grinding out of tune
And time, and cannot find a measure.

But tonight I heard the world's music
Shake hands with itself, old marches
Jazzed into new rhythms, bodhrán
And bones clatter out their resurrection.

So may the world's axis still hold true,
The pole star be constant, our slow
Turning from west to east lead us
Daily from darkness into light.

Waterville, 21st September 2001

Synge's 'Deirdre' on Inis Meán

for Mick Lally

Druid's alchemy again: language gleaming
In astonished revelation, the moon rising
To an occasion centuries in rehearsal,
Stepped ramparts a backdrop where torchlight
Flickers like memory among the stones of the fort.

Here's a rooted man too soon uprooted,
A woman snared in once familiar branches,
The world gashed open by demented power,
Love's unbearable farewell to the unbearable
Betrayal of love and hammering of time.

Dún Chonchúir stands in ovation, the applause
Endless among the high, riveted stars.

Estragon's Boots

for Barry McGovern

Untied. Disembodied. Angled
One against the fallen other,
They could have danced
Or even tottered downstage
To the edge of the darkness
Where orchestras used to play.

Gaping, their tongues swell
In parched silence towards the note
They think they remember, the baton
That held their attention, they think,
Long ago, when they were poised
To step airily into the void.

Tintoretto's Evangelists

The good news is hard work. Inspiration
Gleams in the eyes of lion, ox and eagle,
But waits in the shadows. Only the angel
Leans over Matthew's shoulder to read.

Matthew doesn't notice. Hand and mind
Flow only with the urgencies of text,
Pause only with the pen's momentary pause.
The nimbus around his head is afterthought.

All four, it seems, are on the one word:
Work. And no arty-farty notions of themselves,
Although they hang high up on either side
Of the altar of *Santa Maria del Giglio*.

You mightn't even notice that they write
With their feet fixed firmly in the clouds.

Bear

Was it a curator's hype or a shaman's
Breath misting the glass cases
That gave the name *Art and Magic*
To this exhibition of Eskimo artefacts?

They are ordinary and exquisite
Enough for anything, these figurines
In whale-bone, tusk and driftwood,
Animals and birds of all types, and none.

The Tunit who carved them have vanished
Centuries ago into archaeology
And cannot adjudicate on the catalogue
That says *Bear: floating or flying figure.*

It's easy to see that bone nose
Etching a huge *V* on a mirror of arctic sea.
But flying? And still I share the curator's
Hankering after totems and the journeying of soul.

This is no matter. Art *is* the magic
Of craftsman and shaman, and this bear's
True element is the mind through which it moves
As through a crystal of sea and ice and sky.

II

Forógra

A Dhia is a ghlúinte
Mharfacha na marbh,
Leig dínn. Éirígí
Aníos ónár nguailne
Leis an bhfiach dubh a bhrúigh
Sibh orainn. Leig dúinn
Bheith sinn féin gan bheith
De shíor in bhur bhfiacha-se.
Imígí ag cabaireacht
Le fiacha san uaigneas;
Imígí go dtí an fásach
Ag séideadh bhur dtrumpaí.

Proclamation

Dear God and you deadly
Dead generations,
Enough is enough.
Get off of our backs
Together with the raven
You willed on us. Leave us
To be ourselves, without
The claws of your debt on our shoulders.
Take yourselves cawing
With ravens in the wilderness.
Take yourselves to the desert
To blare on your trumpets.

Counsellor

for Maurice O'Connell

STATUE

You're pedestalled in stone above the traffic,
A bronze statue with attendant figures
Marked by the bullets of civil war.
The city's central street, the bridge

Spanning the coming and going of tides,
Carry your name. O'Connell, Liberator
Counsellor, Dan. It's a long way
From Derrynane to this windy eminence.

Windy's the word they used
There behind you in the G.P.O.
Where poets died strapped to pillars,
Leaving ravens to perch on our shoulders.

But history won't be repealed by you
Or me. Let the hare sit for now.
Emancipated from responsibility,
You can harangue the passing crowds.

FISHING

The boat, lifting with each swell,
Put gunwale to the water as they heaved
The net aboard. Dan helped Galvin
Spill shining mackerel on tarred planks.
After a few shocked, immobile seconds

The drumming started. In an agony
Of convulsion, heads, fins, tails
Hammered the wood. Powerful for salting,
Said Galvin, reaching for the oars.

Dan stared at the striped backs,
The white bellies, the gaping mouths,
All identically helpless. He imagined
The energy of their despair tackled
And driven towards escape. Galvin
Pulled on the oars. The bow lifted.

FOUND POEM

His uncle wrote to Dan's mother:
He is, I am told, employed at visiting
The seats of hares at Kilreelig,
The earths of foxes at Tarmons,
The caves of otters at Bolus,
& the celebration of Miss Burke's wedding at Direen—
useful avocations, laudable pursuits
for a nominal student at law!

MAGEE TRIAL

The Castle prosecuted words, found them
Seditious, libellous of establishments.
Defence abandoned, a strutting upstart
Instead put English law on trial.
You heard the Attorney General
Traduce and calumniate us:
You heard him with patience and temper;
Listen now to our vindication.

Convicting judge, jury and prosecution
He sentenced them to savage mockery
In every town in Ireland. The Counsellor
Had risen to address a different jury.

FOLKLORE AND HISTORY

A story from West Cork has it
That at the time of the Counsellor's birth
The mountains of Kerry echoed
The huge event among themselves.
Torc bellowed over to Mangerton,
Sliabh Mis sang all the way to Brandon,
The Reeks whooped across Bealach Oisín to Carhen.

A modern biography described
His first agitatory meetings:
A distant growl from the hillsides
At last invading Dublin.

Although it may take time,
History can catch up.

DUEL

Cute Kerryman, even unwittingly you managed
To have it both ways. D'Esterrre stalking
Up and down the Four Courts with a whip,
Spluttering about a poltroon in hiding,
Seeded legend. Cúchulainn, Gary Cooper,
Never more effectively, never more reluctantly
Created myth, than you with your single shot.

D'Esterre dead, and your remorse
Became inextricable. We remembered
The immunity to swords and bullets,
The black glove squeezing itself into history.

DAILY WALK

The daily walk from Merrion Square
To the Four Courts became a procession.
The high, wide-brimmed hat, the sweep of cloak
Grew imperial, gathered a train.
'O'Connell's Police', you might say gurriers,
Ensured smooth passage, spontaneous respect.

The walk took half an hour. Once arrived,
Dan would regale the crowd until
O'Connell went inside, opened his law books.

CLARE ELECTION

In Ennis carts creaked under the weight
Of tense watchers. The town spat insults,
Sectarian knives inevitably out,
Threatening the guts of the old order.
The Liberator stood on a platform,
Watching the cabin votes march by
To landlord orders. A raised arm,
A shout to bogs and patches of fields:
Are the freeholders slaves of their landlords?
Brought growling from the ranks. The gentry
Blanched at a force discovering itself.

All the great interests broke down
And the desertion was complete. Peel's words
Made their shocking way to London
While O'Connell was booking his passage.

EVERYBODY KNOWS

Randy old Dan, sure everybody knows
You had women all over Ireland,
And a stone over a workhouse wall
Was sure to hit one of your children.

A pity, says you, it wasn't true.
It might have shortened the long weeks
Away from home on the country's business
When it couldn't even mind its own.
But why let the truth impose itself
On a good story? Sure everybody
Knows you were only superhuman.

PHILOSOPHER

Dissent, roared the bastion,
Is out of the question.

Compromise, screamed the factionry,
Is completely reactionary.

Airiú mo léar, philosophised Dan,
The both of them are all the one.

HUNTING

At Cúm na hEorna, above Derrynane,
Dan rested from the hunt, two hares
Already in the bag. The postman panted
Up the hill. Newspapers, reports
Spread over the rough grass. Gulping milk,
Dan absorbed new splits, fresh alliances.
He chewed breakfast and his options
For the time being, sharpened a knife,
Spat out a mouthful that was stale.
A hare broke wildly from ferns
Reddening with autumn, and streaked
Between heather and furze. Dan howled
Louder than his hounds and careered
For the high ground. From a bluff
He saw the hare take a caol
In its stride then double back
With the pack still straggling across.
Ah you beauty, he whispered and berated
His beagles towards the new course.
Shifting his ground he gave the hare
A clear run for the time being.
That's how it's done, boys, he exulted,
Run with the hare, and hunt with the hounds!
His men were puzzled, but followed his laughter.

BOG

Scum condensed of Irish bog!
Thundered *The Times* from London
At O'Connell. All over Ireland
Bogs continued their slow assimilation

Of leaf, branch and root. Small pools
Winked ambiguously in the sunlight
While heather nodded wisely in the wind.

In Derrynane Dan smiled and spread
His hands towards the turf fire.

CARTOON

The Irish Agitator Tossed by the Papal Bull
Or squatting chained, dogbodied in Richmond Jail,
Apes his uproarious way through *Punch*, *The Times*,
Where *Rint* and *Repale* are pulled across the page by pigs
Driven by *The Big Bull Beggarman, Bishop's Stooge,*
The Real Potato Blight of Ireland.

But this, after all, is everyday stuff
Like Jewish jokes before the Kristallnacht.

LAST SPEECH, FEBRUARY 1847

In the Commons a broken man
Made his last speech for Ireland.
One quarter of the population will perish
Unless you come to her relief.
He swayed as he spoke, and mumbled.

For an old adversary, remembering
The colossal energy which had once
Startled, disturbed and controlled senates,
It was a performance of dumb show.
They stayed silent, out of sympathy.

For two hours the old man rambled
Incomprehensibly about catastrophe.
Only those close to him could hear.

Last Days

In Genoa, death summoned testimony
Incoherent with passion. He raved
Repeal was in a box, denounced
Prime ministers, tabled desperate motions.
Shaking before the judgement, he appealed
For his sentence to be reprieved.
In the end, his agitation ended,
He quietly organised his last days.
Perhaps at last he was satisfied
His brief was well enough prepared.

Ships

The ship that brought home his body,
Berthing at the Custom House, encountered
An emigrant ship escaping famine.

It's said a keening shivered over the water
From one coffin ship to the other.

Imperialisms

Cowardly old Dan, the poets cried,
Was just an empty windbag at Clontarf.
When English cannon called his bluff
He betrayed the imperatives of history
Leaving Ireland to be written by us.

Bloody poets should be locked up
Out of harm's way, O'Connell swore.
Their blasted metaphors became vernacular
Terror, civil war and its bastard politics.
Imperatives of history!
The damned fools simply swapped
One bloody imperialism for another.

OPTIONS

Eternally cute, you kept your options
Open to the end: soul to God,
Heart to Rome, body to Ireland.
The jury was hugely impressed.
Historians say you're being revised
Back again. You'll be seminarred,
God love you, into little pieces.
I'll leave you as I found you,
Towered in Glasnevin, statued in the city,
Hunting storied hares in Derrynane.

Ritual for the Propitiation of the Abnormal Dead

Among the Naxi, the Dongba priests
With flags and images, grain and eggs,
Build a Village of the Abnormal Dead
Where the wandering spirits of those who died
By murder, suicide and war are danced
Into quietude, their village gently destroyed.

I would have them dance all over Ireland,
In towns and villages, and along ditches
Where bodies have been found, and not found.
I would have them dance in Greysteel and in Omagh,
In Monaghan, Soloheadbeg and Kilmainham.
I would have them dance in Enniskillen, Béal na Bláth,
In Ravensdale and Ballyseedy, Talbot Street and Warrenpoint.

I would have them dance every bloody sunday
And weekday until only the everyday
Spirits are abroad for their allotted time,
Before they rest, and let the living live.

Good Friday Assemblage

Here is a new sculpture, not magnificently
Bronze, nor pedestalled on granite.
This is tinkering, gathering, an assemblage.

Here is a bolt coaxed where it doesn't belong,
With exquisite care not to shear the thread.
Here are dirty hands, and coarse cleansing.

This is a sculpture of midnight phonecalls,
Of walk-outs and re-draftings and strategies.
Here's the ache of many twisted arms.

This is a sculpture that has been spun
And doctored and bandaged and splinted.
Here are crutches, oil for hurt egos, cures.

Here are the disposable pens of civil servants
Who rewrite tablets we thought were made of stone.
Here are computers that move words like mountains.

Here are paramilitaries fine-tooth-combing paragraphs,
Teasing out the nuances and defining the parameters
That will allow their heads to stay above the parapet.

Here are the strands too complicated to follow,
And here are the weavers, honoured at last:
Here are the politicians really making shapes.

And the sculptors walk, amazed, around their work,
Not sure of what to say, realising there's no need
For the statues they love to be cast in a furnace.

11 April, 1998

At the Village of the Stone Drum

Shigu. The Stone Drum. On terraced hills
Above the first bend of the Yangtze
The inscription on the great stone wheel
Booms out, across five centuries,

Victory! History! Dynasty! On a nearby hill,
Two heroic figures, soldier and peasant,
Clasp eager hands in newly sculpted memory
Of a river crossed, a retreat transformed.

They are not listening to the drum. They strain
In every sinew towards the end of dynasties.
It is the Long March and the soldier will cross
The Yangtze, and the peasant will help him, and wait.

Their gaze is locked, each in the other,
In a bronze pleading, and a bronze promise,
That the marchers will return across terraces,
Will climb over walls, will scale the dragon's back.

In their eyes too, perhaps, a bronze despair, knowing
That rhythm can be lost in its own hammering,
And the dancing words of a new anthem can stiffen
Into proclamations chiselled on a stone drum.

Models

Mao played a minor role in the First Congress
—Philip Short, *Mao: a life*

The museum on the site of the first
Congress of the Chinese Communist Party
Is reconstructed in the old colonial style.
All of the doorways are granite.

In a wax model, Mao, illuminated
By hindsight, stands and gesticulates.
The lighting is hidden, so that the glow
On his face seems interior, visionary.

The other twelve delegates, just one
Of whom will survive into government,
Hang on every word. They do not notice
The tea-boy who glides between them.

All of the delegates are identified,
Their names engraved near ghostly figures
On a metal plaque. Only the tea-boy,
Who is not listening, remains anonymous.

The Master Calligrapher

He moves easily between styles, absorbing
The character of the times as quickly
As his brush soaks ink. A few strokes
For example, fill the great square
With thousands of faces in an urgent,
Open-ended style, the characters
Simply formed and full of exuberance.

He is equally a master of the older
Clerical script favoured for decrees,
Whose closed and unambiguous characters
Move in unison to surround the square
As marching feet or the tracks of tanks.
Brush poised, he contemplates the final
Balance his manuscript must achieve.

These are the broad strokes. The detail
Is where his controlling genius shows.
Connoisseurs will notice, for example,
How his rendering of the man hidden
Behind screens in the state apartments
Echoes the ideograph of the young man
With arms spread in the path of a tank.

They will notice that the passionate strokes
Delineating the young man's stance and words
Are repeated in a more rigid form to convey
The unheard words and hidden gestures of the other.
They will notice that this subtle change of emphasis
Tightens those outspread arms to a resigned shrug,
And turns a manifesto into a brusque command.

Fuaimrian

Tá sé ag rith is ag ath-rith
Trím aigne: blúire de scannán
Dubh agus bán creathánach
Ar chlár thromchúiseach teilifíse.

Na caogaidí. An tSín. Mao.
An Léim Mhór Chun Tosaigh.
Cruach á bruithniú go craosach
As seanúirlisí i sráidbhailte
Ó cheann ceann na tire,
Agus an ghráin dhearg ag an bPáirtí
Ar éanacha beaga ceoil
As gach aon ghráinne cruithneachtan
A ghoideann siad idir portanna.

Sluaite á mbailiú, mar sin,
Ag gach aon chúinne sráide
Agus bualadh ollmhór oifigiúil bos,
Á spreagadh gan stad le gártha cáinte,
Ag cur na ceoltóirí beaga de gheit
Ag eitilt timpeall agus timpeall arís
Go dtí go dtiteann, ar deireadh, éan
Ar éan de phlimp i ndiaidh a chéile,
Traochta chun báis ar an dtalamh.

Níl aon fhuaimrian ceoil
Leis an scannán. Ach samhlaím
Na mílte fliútanna aeracha bambú
Ag boilgearnach leo scathaimhín,
Agus, poll ar pholl, nóta ar nóta,
Samhlaím gob ollmhór dubh á sárú

Soundtrack

It's rununing and re-running non-stop
In my mind: a small loop of film,
Shaky, black and white,
From some important programme.

The fifties. China. Mao.
The Great Leap Forward.
Steel being hungrily smelted
From scrap in villages
And the Party's official hatred
Of small songbirds
For every last grain of wheat
They steal between tunes.

Crowds being gathered, then,
At every street corner
And a huge sanctioned burst of handclapping
Raising their morale with denunciatory catcalls,
Startling the little songsters into flight
Around and around and around again
Until, in the end, one by one and thud
By thud they fall after each other,
Tired to bits on the ground.

There's no musical soundtrack
To the film. But I imagine
Thousands of giddy bamboo flutes
Bubbling away for a while,
Then, stop by stop, note by note,
One huge black beak cows them
Into silence, one by one.

Chun ciúnais, ceann ar cheann.
Agus samhlaím ina n-áit
Trúmpa mór amháin práis
Ag búireadh an nóta chéanna
Lá i ndiadh lae i ndiaidh lae.

And in their place
One enormous brass trumpet
Bellowing the same note
Day after day after day.

The Paving Stones of Tiananmen Square

They have laid down new paving on Tiananmen Square,
Small armies ceaselessly levelling and barrowing
Along dusty paths and trenches, sweating by day
Under a sun that quivered like a gong, by night
Changing shift for exhausted shift, snatching
A quick smoke near the floodlit, chain-wire fence.

The blank verse of the five great arches,
Below the genial portrait, anticipates
The marching feet, the trundling tanks
That will proclaim the anniversary
Whose stately and implacable rhythms echo
Across the measured paving stones by day.

The lyrical, on the other hand, comes out by night
And strolls among the families around the square,
Where fluttering kites blossom like flowers
And a hundred strings contend for space,
Inching towards a level where butterflies and dragons
Can soar above stones that are smooth and unstained.

July 1999

In the Summer Palace

for Hu Xiang Qun

Towards the century's turn, the Dowager Empress
With her ladies and attendant eunuchs promenades
Across the seventeen perfectly spaced arches
Of a sun-dazed bridge, between summer rains.

Shaded by parasols and willow branches,
They scatter crumbs among carp and goldfish,
Discovering constantly new perspectives
Westward, towards The Fragrant Hills.

Along the great bends of the Yangtse,
The yellow, eroded clay collapses
Inexorably into landslides,
And oozes towards the swollen river

That will burst its banks again this year
As the scarred, exhausted mountains
Steel themselves against the rain
And ache for their forest roots.

They pass the Hall of Literary Prosperity,
Where, delicately, for fear of damage,
Scholars in silk robes unwind scrolls,
Calligraphing the art of government.

Outside, an ox cast in bronze
Chews the cud of many centuries,
Her placid reflection in the lake
A totem against threatened floods.

All across the provinces, dragons blink
To find themselves pulling railway cars,
While words like imperial *and* dynasty
Are striking a different note in the streets.

In the stinking alleys, in the lecture-halls,
In villages along the terraced hills,
Ideas throb like cicadas, sing like caged birds
And flow like endless cups in teahouses.

Along the colonnade of the Long Corridor,
They admire painting after exquisite painting
Of myth and dynasty and history, a path
That leads them to a pavilion by a pond,

Where, soothed by their peacock-feather fans,
And schooled to trace the music in a poem,
The ladies sit and pattern the sound
Of raindrops, falling on the lotus leaves.

Work Done

i.m. Michael Moynihan

A phrase from the doorsteps comes to mind,
Dusted off and renewed like an old poster
Repeating itself from pole to pole:
Sure Mike's a gentleman, we won't forget him.

God knows you were easy to canvass for,
And when you outpaced the door-knockers
Around an estate, you were easily followed
As you forged ahead, tall and upright.

Forty years approaching many doors,
And now you've reached the last threshold.
But there's no need to canvass any further,
Because it's like you always said yourself:

If work done counts, your seat
Among the elect is safe as houses.

Aniar Aduaidh

Aniar aduaidh a thiocfaidh sé, an Díle nua,
Beag beann ar Dhia, tubaist dár rogha féin.
Fillfidh ar bhfeall orainn, mall nó luath.

Teas marfach isea feasta an aimsir chrua.
Soineann ina doineann, na séasúir ina gcíreib.
Aniar aduaidh a thiocfaidh sé, an Díle nua.

Goin croí na cruinne, agus fágfar í gan trua.
Meileann oighearshruth go mall, ach meileann go mín réidh.
Fillfidh ár bhfeall orainn, mall nó luath.

Tá geonaíl an oighir ag rá go bhfuiltear chugainn,
Sinn sna críocha déanacha, ag tús is deireadh ré.
Aniar aduaidh a thiocfaidh sé, an Díle nua.

Baoth anois bheith ag cuardach, baoth bheith ag súil
Le hÁirc ár gConartha le sainnt, conradh nimhnithe an aeir.
Fillfidh ár bhfeall orainn, mall nó luath.

Coimhthíoch a bheifear, ar nós chine aduain
A fhágfar gan tórramh, gan uaigh, gan chré.
Aniar aduaidh a thiocfaidh sé, an Díle nua,
Fillfidh ár bhfeall orainn, mall nó luath.

Out of the Blue

The new Flood will surge, Godless, out of the blue
From the northwest, a judgement all our own.
Our broken faith will turn on us, late or soon.

Warmth has grown deadly now, sunlight is gloom,
The calm is the storm, the seasons overthrown.
The new Flood will surge, Godless, out of the blue.

Wound the world's heart, and she will no longer rue
The glacier grinding slowly, but grinding to the bone.
Our broken faith will turn on us, late or soon.

The groaning ice announces our impending doom,
The end and start of cycles, a metamorphic zone.
The new Flood will surge, Godless, out of the blue.

Too late now for searching, awaiting like fools
Our Ark of Covenant with greed, our air-poisoning hoard.
Our broken faith will turn on us, late or soon.

Our end will be alien, an abandoned crew
Without wake, without grave, without marking stone.
The new Flood will surge, Godless, out of the blue
And our broken faith turn on us, late or soon.

Búireadh

Beireann oighearshruth lao, adeirtear,
Nuair a scoilteann meall oighir go callánach
Amach uaithi, agus féach ansin romham
Fíord fairsing agus é breac le laonna bána,
A gceann fúthu, ag iníor go suaimhneach
Ar mhachairí míne méithe an tsáile,
Ar ghoirt ghorma ghoirte na farraige.

Ach cad é an búireadh sin a chuala
I gcoim na hoíche aréir, slua-bhúireadh
Mar a bheadh tréad i bpéin? B'shin búir
Oighearchlár mátharach an tréada
Ag lobhadh i dteas buile na cruinne,
Ag cúbadh is ag cúngú is ag leá
I ndeora goirte sáile ár máthar uile.

Bellowing

A glacier calves, the expression has it,
When an iceberg moves noisily
Away out from her. And look: before my eyes
A huge fiord dappled with white calves,
Heads down, grazing peacefully
On the smooth, salubrious saline plains,
On the blue, briny fields of the ocean.

But what was that bellowing I heard
In the dead of last night, a mass bellowing
Like a herd in pain? That was the bellowing
Of the herd's maternal icecap
Rotting in the crazed heat of the globe,
Straining and shrinking and melting
In the bitter salt tears of the universal mother.

Giorria Artach

Id staic i logán sléibhe, do dhá chluas
Ar bior, d'fheadfá bheith san airdeall
Ar ghlam gadhar i ngleannta Uíbh Ráthaigh,
Ach go scéitheann dath aolbhán do chóta

Gur sneachta an tuaiscirt is dual agus dúchas duit.
Nó an é an bainne a ghoid an chailleach,
Á dhiúl i riocht ghiorria ó bhuaibh na gcomharsan,
A chlaochlaigh thú go gile sin na gcríoch seo?

Cuma sa tsioc. San iarghúltacht chrua seo
Leánn agus reonn rógaireacht agus leochaileacht
Tríd is tríd a chéile, beag beann ar chora
Tromchúiseacha an tsaoil. Teacht slán is cúram.

Tásc ná tuairisc níl agamsa le coicíos
Ar an saol mór ná ar chinnithe na bhfear
A labhrann le Dia is a labhrann Dia leo
Roimh scaoileadh na mbuamaí, roimh an gol san ár.

Ach ó tá an domhan mar ghiorria idir chonartaibh,
Gach aon bhall ar crith, ag éisteacht faoi sceimhle
Le séideadh adhairce na sealgairí mire
Ar shliabh is ar mhachaire is ar fhásach,

Seo mo ghuí do ghiorria i logán sléibhe sa Ghraonlainn:
Fiolar, faolchú ná ulcabhán nár thaga ort,
Crobh, gob ná fiacal nár ruga riamh ort,
Is ná raibh do chlúmh bhán choíche breac led fhuil.

Arctic Hare

Transfixed in a mountain hollow, your ears
All attention, you could be listening out
For baying beagles in Uíbh Ráthach valleys,
But that your lime-white coat can't hide

That northern snow is in your blood and breeding.
Or is it that the milk the old witch, taking
The shape of a hare, stole from the neighbours' cows,
Has you morphed into this indigenous brightness?

No matter. In this unyielding remoteness,
Villainy and vulnerability meld one
Into the other, undisturbed by the weighty
Ways of the world. Survival's the thing.

For two weeks now, I've had neither sight nor sound
Of the big world, nor of the decrees of men
Who speak to God and to whom God speaks
Before the bombs' release, the weeping in the slaughter.

But since the world is now a hare between packs,
Trembling in every part, listening in terror
To the bugling of the crazed hunters
Among mountains and plains and deserts,

Here is my wish for this hare in a Greenland hollow:
May no wolf nor owl nor eagle come upon you,
May no tooth nor beak nor talon tear you,
And may your white fur never be dappled with blood.

Áireamh na nDeachúna

Ar phár a tháinig slán chugainn ón mbliain
D'aois ár dTiarna míle dhá chéad ochtó, taispeántar
Gur sheol Eaglais Lochlannach na Graonlainne
Deachúna Crosáide go dtí Pápa na Róimhe
I riocht míle ceithre chéad seachtó punt éibhir
De starrfhiacla céad nócha is a haon bhálrus
A ghnóthaigh fiche sé phunt d'airgead geal glan.

Nár dheachúna iad san! Fiacla fada géara
Á stracadh as cloigne na rón is á seoladh
Ón dTuaisceart reoite go dtí an tOirthear loiscneach,
Fiacla geala Críostaí ag réabadh doircheacht Ioslaim,
Fiacla dragúin á gcur sa ghaineamh, ag síolrú
Fómhar fola atá fós á bhaint, deachúna
Á n-íoc agus á n-aisíoc arís ina milliúnta.

Reckoning the Tithes

On a parchment that has come down to us
From the year of Our Lord twelve hundred and eighty,
It is recounted that the Norse Church of Greenland
Sent Crusade Tithes to the Pope of Rome
In the form of one thousand four hundred and seventy pounds
Of ivory from the tusks of one hundred and ninety-eight walrus
Which realised twenty-six pounds of pure bright silver.

Was not that some tithing! Long sharp teeth
Torn from the walrus heads and dispatched
From the frozen North to the burning East,
Bright Christian teeth ripping the darkness of Islam,
Dragons' teeth sown in the desert, seeding
A bloody harvest still being reaped, tithes
Being paid and repaid again in their millions!

Not Adlestrop

No. I don't remember the name—
Something European. But when the train
Drew in there unexpectedly last year
The people seemed familiar just the same.

It was summer. The high walls
Had been levelled to make space
For stalls and offices. From everywhere
Crowds hurried to the rebuilt marketplace.

In the train, people were singing,
Making up words as they went along.
On the platform, soldiers stumbled
Through an older, half-remembered song.

And at that minute the mortars coughed
Close by, and circled nearer
And nearer, around the nameless towns
Of Bosnia, and Herzegovina.

Lie Detector

I

The polygrapher's electrodes probing
Glandular secretions have spoken
To antennae which have traced
On screens and paper the evidence
Which leads to a conclusion which
Mirrors the pulse of conscience.
    This machine is beyond belief.

II

The polygrapher questioned history:
The priests on holy wars,
The princes on discontent,
The generals on casualties,
The politicians on starvation,
The philosophers on systems,
The artists on their families,
The merchants on the world's soul.
    Their answers raised not a flicker
    Of incredulity in the machine.

91

III

An old man with only sunlight
Beneath his wrinkled eyelids
Swore the desert floor once blossomed
Into a canticle of itself.
   The graph grew long spikes,
   Became a cactus of disbelief.
The jagged ups and downs of untruth
Are contained within reasonable bounds
Of the machine. It will not plunge
To the underworld nor judge the messages
Of men descending from the mountain.
   Orpheus, therefore, and Moses
   Are deemed inconclusive.

IV

The truth floats by on an even keel
Without revelation. Only falsehood
Lurches wildly in shocked waves.
This is the polygrapher's ache: to find
Patterns only in the detection of lies.
   Inquisitors beside the rack,
   Policeman in basement cells,
   Judges of dissent, all guardians
   In good faith of all common goods
   Sniffing deviation must likewise thirst
   For truth also to scream its secrets.

VI

And whisper it, whisper, does it—
Strapped to his own terminals—could he
Detect his own small patterns
And bear to reflect himself?
      O pity all polygraphers!
      On screens, in mirrors
      The truth lies before their eyes.

Full Moon, 18 March 2003

The moon rises over Binn Mhór,
Clarifying the far
And wide world
In silver and black.

This moon is not crescent
Or fertile. It is a desert moon
Preparing to explode, a shell
About to fragment itself
Into craters, sockets, skulls.

This moon still hears gods
Commanding their own
Deaths and resurrections.

This moon is a new century
Howling at itself.

This moon knows its real colours
Full well: pitch-black,
Blood-red, gold.

This moon yearns
To gild minarets.

Now it trembles
Over the dark horizon
Like an unshed tear.

During the Bombing of Baghdad

And I remember, at Macleod's Stone,
On a stunning day in Harris last June,
How the bomber howled down out of the blue
Precisely towards the stone, and how the air
Trembled in awe and shock as it climbed
Again and curved up and away to plot
A course for another practice run.
And it was just one plane and dropped no bomb.

And I remember a different day in Harris,
Years ago, when I saw for the first time,
Furtive in a scythed meadow, a corncrake
Dappled with its own camouflage, the hay
Ablaze with meadow-flowers and sunlight.
And I think of those shy, resonant birds
Circling in blind panic as mowing machines snarl
Around the shrinking centre of the field.

15 April, 2003

Now the sky has disintegrated,
The stars are clustered like bombs,
And words of mass destruction
Howl at the crescent moon.

Now truth's an unspoken whisper
Embedded in powerful lies,
And justice a streak of vengeance
Howling through smoke-filled skies.

Now history's a looted city
Whose charter's disfigured and torn,
And Christ's on a zealot's banner
Wishing he'd never been born.

Now evil has developed an axis
That stretches from pole to pole,
And a Faustian superpower
Lays claim to the whole world's soul.

Now government meets in the market
Where statesmen have oily tongues,
And reason is drowned in the babble
Of merchants displaying their guns.

And what will the merchants be selling
When they've left us no water or bread,
When all that is left will be desert
And oil to embalm the dead?

The Minister's Holiday Home

for Pat Compton

The minister's three-and-a-half-storey
Holiday home at a bend of the river
Rises like a capital "I" lording it
Over the lower case, or like a tower-house
Planted by some dark foreigner to instil
Obeisance and right attitudes in its surrounds.

As our boat noses upriver, we wonder
If we should pay tribute, even a nominal toll,
To chug past the magisterial ramparts
Of this *seigneur du droit*. Instead, we bow to its stern
Proclamations of right thinking, and swing left
Under a bridge into a welcome haven.

The water, tributary only to its own flowing,
A nibbling ground for coot and waterhen and duck,
Is unperturbed as it moves downstream,
Its currents and its eddies comprehending
Within themselves how time and weather deal
With ramparts, with dogma, and with proclamations.

*Dark foreigner: from the Irish dubh-ghall, which gives us
surnames such as Doyle, McDowell etc.*

III

Amergin was the seer and lawgiver of the Celtic invaders who first landed at Ballinskelligs Bay in Kerry. At the moment of landing, Amergin chanted a song in which he claimed identity with the surrounding land and water. Scéine was Amergin's wife, Érannán and Donn his brothers.

Freagra Scéine ar Aimhirghin

Más tusa gaoth na mara
      Is mé an fharraige om shearradh féin faoid leoithne
Más tonn díleann thú
      Is sliogán folamh mé ag tnúth led theacht
Más tú gáir na stoirme
      Is mé lapadaíl na taoide i mbrothall nóna
Más damh seacht mbeann thú
      Tiocfad go mánla chugat ar aiteann
Más seabhac thú ar an bhfaill
      Beannód thú le liricí fuiseogacha
Más deoir drúchta faoin ngréin thú
      Brúfad féar na maidne leat
Más tú is áille a fhásann
      Bláthód leat bliain ar bhliain
Más torc ar mire thú
      Cuirfead geasa gháire ar na fiacla fada agat
Más bradán thú sa linn
      Meallfad cuileoga ina gcéadta chugat
Más loch ar mhá thú
      Raghad go tóin poill ionat
Más tú rún na héigse
      Mise na naoi mBéithe agat
Má bhíonn faobhar ort chun troda
      Cuirfead ceangal na ceanúlachta ort
Má bhíonn tinfeadh á adhaint sa cheann agat
      Séidfead síol na tine duit

Tá fhios ag mo chroí istigh cé réitigh an bealach dom,
Cé ba réalt eolais, cé bhronn grian agus gealach orm,
Is in ainneoin na gcloch seo, agus an solas ag dul in éag,
Mairfead scáth ar scáth leat, focal ar fhocal leis an ngaoth.

21 Nollaig 1999, ag uaigh Scéine

100

Scéine's Reply to Amergin

If you are the wind on the sea
     I am the water tingling under your breeze
If you are a wave in flood
     I am an empty shell dreaming of your coming
If you are the roar of a storm
     I am the tide lapping in the noon heat
If you are the stag of seven horns
     I will pick my way to you gracefully through furze
If you are a hawk on the cliff
     I will bless you with lyrics of larksong
If you are a dewdrop in the sun
     I will bruise the morning grass with you
If you are the fairest of flowers
     I will blossom year upon year with you
If you are a maddened boar
     I will charm your tusks into laughter
If you are a salmon in the pool
     I will lure infinities of insects to you
If you are a lake in the plain
     I will plumb your very depths
If you are the essence of poetry
     I am all of your muses
If you are edging towards a fight
     I will bewitch you to bluntness
If you are kindling inspiration in the mind
     I will blow on the seed of the fire for you

I know in my heart who made the way smooth for me,
Was a star of knowledge for me, gave the sun and moon to me,
And though the stones close in, and light moves towards its end,
We will shadow one another, word for word with the wind.

21 December 1999, at the grave of Scéine

Labhrann Érannán

Mise i dtosach a chonaic, naoi dtonn amach,
Crochta in airde ar chrann seoil na loinge,
An tír mar thairngireacht romham ós cionn an cheo.
Ach ba ag an neomat gur scaoileas uaim an gháir

Gur ghabh creathán grod ó thosach deireadh na cíle,
Gur bhris an crann, gur caitheadh siar amach
Ar chúl mo chinn ar an gcarraig mé, gur slogadh
Isteach sa tsáile mé, gur idirshaolaíodh mé

Im neach farraige ar charraig cois cósta,
Im aonarán féachana, im aonarán éisteachta
Ag an dul i dtír agus ag gach a d'eascair as:
Deasghnátha, tithe agus glór páistí ar an dtrá.

Chuala uaim iad, an bád ag siosarnach
Suas ar an ngaineamh, an liú caithréimeach,
Torann na rámha á dtarraingt ar bord,
An fuadar chun chladaigh, agus focla tromchúiseacha

Mo dhearthár ag scaothaireacht leis gurbh é
Féin an ghaoth, féin an seabhach, féin an bradán,
Féin an uile ní beo ar bith, agus neamhbheo—
Siúd ná mairfeadh trí lá ar an gcarraig seo,

Le báirnigh á scríobadh, faoileáin á chiapadh,
Agus gan ach cleasaíocht focal mar scáth aige
Seachas dúire sin na carraige atá anois buanaithe
Go docht im aigne. Mar is gá dom. Mar is fuath liom.

Érannán Speaks

It was I who first saw it, across nine waves
From my perch high in the rigging,
The land like a prophecy over the mast.
But it was on the very instant I yelled out

That the keel shook from stem to stern,
The mast split, I was flung out
On my head on the rock, was swallowed
Back into the saltwater, was otherworlded

As a sea being on a coastal rock,
A lone witness, a lone listener
To the landing and to all that ensued:
Ceremonies, houses and children's voices on the beach.

I heard it from a distance, the boats whispering
Up onto the sand, the huge fanfaronade,
The clamorous shipping of the oars,
The scramble onto shingle, and the ponderous words

Of my brother windbagging that he himself
Was wind and wave, was hawk and salmon,
Was all being that lived, and did not—
Himself who wouldn't last three days on this rock,

Harrowed by limpets, tormented by gulls,
With only the trickery of words to shelter him
Instead of the rocky stubbornness now petrified
Firmly in my soul. My essence. My hate.

Tonn i ndiaidh toinne om bhascadh, om thachtadh
Le cúr mire mar a bheadh bainne cíche na Baidhbhe,
Om bheathú chun báis, is an fheamainn ghoirt
Om lascadh gan staonadh chun beatha arís.

Mhaíodar gur cuireadh thall mé, le Scéine,
Ansiúd ar an gcnoc, faoi chlocha arda
Chun mé a threorú chun gealaigh agus gréine
Maíomh chomh folamh leis an uaigh féin.

Conas a chuirfí nach raibh ann le cur?
Mo chorp i smidiríní spéire agus farraige,
Gan chliabhán, gan uaigh, scoite amach ar charraig
Idir chósta mo dhúchais agus cósta mo mhéine.

Níor leagas mo chos ar thalamh úr, níor chanas
Aon fhocal a mhaireann, níor ghabhas seilbh
Ar aon dúthaigh, níor luadh aon scéal liom
Ach mar a bheadh iarmhír ann, nó as.

Táim níos faide siar ná cuimhne na ndaoine,
Ann ar éigin ar Charraig Éanna. Ach éist:
Tá mianach sa charraig, lá i ndiaidh lae,
Ná faightear sa bhfoclaíocht is buaine ar bith.

Wave after wave battering me, choking me
With crazed foam like the breast milk of the Fury,
Nurturing death in me, then the bitter seaweed
Whipping me relentlessly to life again.

They claimed I was buried there with Scéine,
Over there on the hill, under standing stones
To direct me towards the sun and the moon—
A claim as empty as the grave itself.

How can you bury what is not there to be buried?
My body fragmented into sea and sky,
Without cradle, without grave, outcast on a rock
Between my native shore and the shore of my longing.

I did not set foot on new land, did not sing
Any words that lasted, did not appropriate
Any territory, played no part in stories
But as an afterword, neither here nor there.

I go back further than race memories,
Barely there on Carraig Éanna. But listen:
There is mettle in the rock, day after day,
Not found in the longest of long-lasting words.

Labhrann Donn

Is mise dorchadas m'ainm féin,
An taobh thall den ngealach,
Deireadh báire na gile,
Tóin an mhála fáiscithe.
Is mé a mhúchann an dé deiridh.

Formad le mo dheártháir, adúradar,
A tharraing mí-ádh orainn araon,
Sea, agus cíochras míchuíosach chun troda
Ba chúis nár roinneadh Éire liom.
Bladar. Fuath do ghach aon neach beo
Agus cíochras chun féasta na gcnuimh
Is bun le mo ríocht. Agus féach!
Éire gan roinnt ag triall ar mo thigh-se.

Donn na Duimhche. Teach Duinn.
Níl cion ar ainm an oileáin.
Luaitear tarbh liom, bó agus lao faram.
Bídís ag iníor tamall.

Ní thagann iascairí im ghaobhar
Ar eagla a slogtha scun scan
Ins na roithleáin timpeall orm.
Ach tá traimilí foighne agam,
Agus línte ná briseann.

Tá tigh solais ar an oileán
Agus dord a fhógraíonn ceo.
Ach slogaimse dríodar gach solais
Agus sním mar cheo trí phollairí na marbh.

Tá mo chapall cloiste agat
Go doimhin san oíche. Téanam go luath
Ag marcaíocht ar na dumhacha.

Donn Speaks

I am the darkness of my own name,
The far side of the moon,
The final end of brightness,
The narrowing cul de sac.
It is I who chokes off the last breath.

Envy of my brother, they said,
Brought bad luck to both of us,
Yes, and an inordinate bloodthirst
Meant no part of Ireland was for me.
Bullshit. Hatred towards all living beings
And a thirst for the feasting of worms
Is my right of kingship. And look!
The whole of Ireland travels towards my house.

Donn of the Dunes. Donn's House.
The name of the island is not liked.
I am known as a bull, a cow and a calf near me.
Let them graze awhile.

Fisherman don't approach me
For fear they'd be swallowed whole
In the maelstrom around me.
But I have trammels of patience
And cords that will not break.

There is a lighthouse on the island
And a horn that trumpets fog.
But I swallow the dregs of all light
And I flow like a mist through the nostrils of the dead.

You have heard my horse
Deep into the night. Come with me soon
Riding on the dunes.

Athdhán Aimhirghin

ag oscailt oifigiúil Tech Amergin, 27 Deireadh Fómhair, 2006

Mé túr os cionn ceardlanna
Mé gallán i measc crann
Mé aisling nár shearbhaigh
Mé pictiúr ar fhalla bán
Mé ríomhaire ag idirlíonú
Mé bean ag adhmadóireacht
Mé fear ag dearadh síoda
Mé ceol agus oiliúint ceoil
Mé saothar agus a luach
Mé cré na bpotadóirí
Mé aitheasc an Aire
Mé dathanna dhalta ar chanbhás
Mé dealbhóireacht adhmaid
Me iliomad teangacha
Mé drama ar stáitse
Mé turas seandalaíochta
Mé féile le fáilte fial
Mé géagshíneadh yoga
Mé teacht le chéile seanóirí
Mé céim damhsa
Mé súíl, croí agus inchinn ealaíontóra

Cé a chuirfidh tús nó deireadh liom?
Cé a thomhasfaidh mo dhoimhneas nó m'airde?
Cé a déarfas an óg nó aosta mé?
Cé a déarfas an fireann nó baineann mé?
Cé a leomhfas aon teora a chur liom?

Mé Aimhirghin, beo in athuair.
Scáil na háite tógtha, mairim arís.
Mé Aimhirghin Glúingheal: fáilte chun mo thí-se.

Amergin Rewrites

at the official opening of Tech Amergin, 27 October 2006

I am a tower over workshops
I am a standing stone among trees
I am a dream that did not sour
I am a painting on a white wall
I am a computer internetting
I am a woman at woodwork
I am a man decorating silk
I am music and its teaching
I am the work and its worth
I am the potters' clay
I am the Minister's speech
I am the student's colours on canvas
I am sculpture in wood
I am many languages
I am a play on the stage
I am an archaeological walk
I am a festival of generous welcome
I am the stretching limbs of yoga
I am the gathering of elders
I am a step of a dance
I am the eye, heart and mind of an artist

Who will decide my beginning or my end?
Who will measure my height or my depth?
Who will say that I am old or young?
Who will say that I am male or female?
Who will dare to set my limits?

I am Amergin, reincarnated.
The shadow lifted from the place, I live once more.
I am Amergin Glúingheal: welcome to my house?

Poems with Amergin

The Bay

The sea has its pastures.

I remember, at our entrance
To the bay, the ruminative seals
Raised acquiescent heads, bowed again
Towards rich shoals. Oystercatchers,
Merry among the thrift,
Promised mussels, urchins.

Abundance ratified our course.
Journey became procession.

Porpoises attended us,
Exhaling benedictions, undulating
Ceremonious welcomes. Curious
Gannets wove auspicious patterns.

Inevitably, possessively, our prows
Slid onto the shingle.

The Song

It is still
My song. I claim
Kinship with the place
And all its additions. Especially
The additions. In which I exist,
Without whom I never existed,
Nor will.

I remember
We laid claim to the bay.
The shore, the woods. Above all,
The lake. These were claimed
In words of mine which afterwards
Grew holy, as the woods were cleared.
Trees fell, seeds grew and words
Were added to our claim,
Became words which have always been.
(If this puzzles,
Examine other words which still
Cast weapons and seem
As if they always have been.
Mine, at least,
Intending no harm,
Inclined towards light.)

THE LAKE

It may be that I now understand
How the necessity of fish and fowl,
Water and the sanctuary
Of small islands, invested the lake
With an unreal immanence. This I understand,
Recollecting all that I know; but
Recollecting also that the wind
Racing over its shadow spoke
With more than its own breath;
Or that clouds in procession
Across its summer surface
Were a reflection of more than themselves.

THE PRICE

Place can lie heavy
On the soul. Because
Of the blood-price paid
To the place, we became
The place. My brothers, for example:
One flung from the look-out mast
When the nearness of the place
Swallowed familiar caution. I mean
That the reef which killed him holds still his name. I mean
Another, drowned, who named the island
Where we sent our dead. I mean
The dolmen of the dead queen,
Near the lake where she bathed
With such new delight. I mean
That those killed in skirmishes
(It was an easy invasion) held
The place with us.

I mean everything this led to:
The persistent naming of holy places,
The dead continuing their constant invasions.

QUESTION

Amergin, a rowan tree now
Decorates my father's garden.
The wind and moon, voiceless,
Lie pinned among charts.
Your cauldron lake, its salmon,
Are plumbed, tagged. How,
In an inanimate time, will
Fire ignite in the head, or light
Be thrown on the mountain?

Amergin smiled, turned, became
A hare on the mountain.
Below, beagles negotiated a wire fence.

ALIGNMENTS

Amergin, old pebble in the brain,
Stone is not silent.

Those still articulate
Lichened monuments recall
How you portioned out the sky
And the seasons. The sun itself
Must have seemed to answer
To your great stones, which spread
Like huge questions along the hills,
Seeking to align equinox with solstice,
Now with then, and the dead
With the living. And what else
Is there to search for now,
When blinded men, driven
By the dead, would wrench
The wheel of the sun from its axle?
Simply to form the question
Is almost to answer,
And not to question
Will lead us, chanting,
Towards lunar fastnesses.

Listen to the old
Articulacy of stone.

Aimhirghin ar an iPod

do Patrick Cassidy, ceoltóir, agus Lisa Gerrard, amhránaí

Nuair a luigh na 30 GBanna
Go slim sleamhain ciardhubh im láimh,
Shíleas ná tiocfainn choíche go dtína mbun
Ná a mbarr as mo stuaim féin
Is ná féadfadh fiú sliocht mo shleachta
Croí na mistéire a thabhairt chun solais.

Ach, mar a bhí ráite liom sna treoracha,
Thosnaíos ag an tús agus ar deireadh
D'éirigh liom *The Song of Amergin*
A íoslódáil as an aer, agus thumas
Go doimhin sna cluasáin, ag éisteacht
Le maorgacht an cheoil shintéisigh
Agus ársaíocht focal an fhile úd
A tháinig i dtír im aigne i bhfad ó shin.

Shiúlaíos liom ar thaobh na farraige
Agus go doimhin isteach sna sléibhte,
Ag éisteacht le glór gaoithe ar muir
       le glam toinne in anfa
       le scread seabhaigh ar fhaill
       le búireamh damh ar bheannaibh
       le léimt is titim bradán i loch
       le dord beiche i mbéal blátha
       le gáir fiaigh i gcoim sléibhe
       le ceileabhair fuiseog os cionn aitinn
       le fiántas focal an fhile
Chun tosnú, mar atá ráite,
Glan amach ag an tús.

Amergin on the iPod

for Patrick Cassidy, composer, and Lisa Gerrard, singer

When all thirty GB's of it
Lay smooth and black and slender in my hand,
I thought I would never even begin
To get it together in my own head
And that even my own children couldn't
Enlighten me about its mysterious heart.

But, as I had been instructed, I read
Right from the beginning and in the end
I managed to download *The Song of Amergin*
From the air, and I dived
Deep into the earphones, listening
To the majesty of that synthesis
And to the ancient words of that poet
Who long ago made landfall in my mind.

I walked by myself beside the sea
And deep into the mountains
Listening to the wind's voice on the sea
          to the baying wave in a storm
          to the hawk's screech on a cliff
          to stags bellowing on the hills
          to salmon leaping and falling in a lake
          to a bee droning in the mouth of a flower
          to the raven's croak among mountains
          to the celebration of larks over furze
          to the wild words of the poet
In order to begin, as has been said,
Right at the very beginning.

Leagan Eile

i ndiaidh Aimhirgin

Is mé gaoth na mara
      Mo neart tomhaiste ag saitilítí
Is tonn díleann mé
      A saolaíodh trí pholl sa spéir
Is mé gáir na stoirme
      Atá á fógairt le ráithe
Is beithíoch gan adharc mé
      Le páipéirí mar is cuí
Is deoir drúchta faoin ngréin mé
      Ollmhéadaithe ag ceamara
Is mé is áille a fhásann
      Faoi chosaint ar eagla mo chaillte
Is torc chun giniúna mé
      Faoi chuing ráillí iarainn
Is bradán feirme mé
      I mbéal Inbhear Scéine
Is loch ar mhá mé
      Ag slogadh dríodar na talamhaíochta
Is mé croí na saíochta
      Idirlíonta le h-eolas
Bíonn faobhar orm chun chatha
      Le buama i lár baile
Adhnaim tinfeadh sa cheann
      De réir rialacha na loighice

Cé leis an t-innealra a dheineann réidh na garbhchríocha?
Cé aige atá a fhios cá bhfuil deannach na gealaí?
Agus a fhógraíonn éiclipseanna na gréine?
Cé a lasann an spéir oíche gan réalthainn?
Agus gur eol dó go smior nádúr an tinnis?

Cloisim, gan tuiscint, caoineadh na gaoithe.

Another Version

after Aimhirgin

I am the wind on the sea
    My strength measured by satellite
I am a wave in flood
    Born of a hole in the sky
I am the roar of a storm
    That has been forecast for months
I am a beast without horns
    With my papers in order
I am a dewdrop in the sun
    Magnified by a camera
I am the fairest of flowers
    Protected against extinction
I am a boar for breeding
    Penned in with railings
I am a salmon in a farm
    At the mouth of Inbhear Scéine
I am a lake in the plain
    Swallowing the dregs of agriculture
I am the heart of wisdom
    Internetted by knowledge
I am edging towards battle
    With a bomb in a town centre
I kindle inspiration in the mind
    Following the laws of logic

Who owns the machinery that makes the rough smooth?
Who knows where the dust of the moon is
And forecasts exactly eclipses of the sun?
Who lights up the sky on a night without stars
And knows in his marrow the nature of illness?

I hear, without understanding, the lamentation of the wind.

IV

After Love

for Fiona

The cockle relaxes its grip. Small creatures,
Like nerves on the estuary of our bodies,
Settle again, and discover once more
Their oozing world, as the tide recedes.

The frantic seaweed, stilled now,
Only half regrets the small rivulets
Still trickling, unpractised, towards the sea.
The small sat-grassed islands can forget

The surge and swell that joined them
And go back to just being islands,
For the time being, and the space being,
To ring and ring and ring in silence.

A lark is climbing through octaves of the sky
To celebrate us, high and dry.

Occasional Poem

What should it be, this occasional poem
For our wedding's twentieth anniversary?
Can it absorb the phrase, its casual solemnity,
Record the day without a stiffened pose?

Annus versus. The years have turned
Kindly around our marriage. Increasingly,
Patterns form of themselves. Behind the creaking
Of the world's works, the spheres still hum

And drum the rhythm of our days. This
Is the everyday poem of our marriage
Rewriting itself, revising arguments,
Sounding us out with different emphases.

So day by day and line by line we write
Ourselves, occasionally in almost perfect rhyme.

Postcard from Hospital

Just a few post-observation lines to say
Your diagnosis was spot-on. All samples,
Syringes, charts and consultants now confirm
The diabetes you nagged so patiently about.

So this is just to thank you, and your blood's
Worth bottling too. Forgive the sour words.
All I could hear was a threatening buzz
And, shying from imagined stings,

I slapped uselessly at myself, forgot
The rich slow dripping in the comb.
Now I must find a new path to the hive
And savour every taste along the way.

I'll be home soon, complete with my prognosis,
Craving mouth upon mouthful of your sweetness.

Portrait of a Woman Sewing

Again, tonight, as in a Dutch painting,
You lean towards the illuminated intricacies
Of your machine. On the floor, paper
Pinned to fragrant cloth, whispers

Of bolero jackets, and skirts that might
Brush the dew from feathery grasses,
Or lift themselves knowingly over barbed wire,
While the children run ahead, laughing.

In the front room of your mother's house—
Ages ago, remember?—the mysteries
Of bust and hips we figured out,
Immersed in new patterns, new dresses.

And, sometimes, while waiting scissors gaped,
We inched towards the real thing.

A Dream of Lapwings

All day, as we walked the island,
Lapwings cavorted in the wind, or carried
Their crested silhouettes from rock to rock,
Mewing between heather and sheep-cropped grass.

You once dreamed, you said, of a great lapwing
That with huge wingbeats and rippling plumage
Carried you high over familiar mountains
While you clung to the iridescence of its crest.

Later, as we lay drowsily
High among the cliff-top buttercups,
Lapwings in high-pitched abandon above us
Played your dream again. I could see

The hugeness of your flight above a valley,
How it brought people streaming out of doors
To marvel at the shadow, and to feel
The beneficence of those passing wings.

The Poet Pines in Exile in Suzhou

The neon sky is sodden with mist tonight,
Discoloured as the canals that carry
Plastic bags under stepped stone bridges
In ornamental gardens. Here scribes and poets
Wrote elegantly of absent friends and distant wives.

Leaves that should compose their own calligraphy
Of loneliness under a clarifying moon
Are limp in its absence. Even poor Li Bai
Had his own shadow to keep him company
And with him raise a wine-cup to the moon.

My shadow lies within myself. And so
I spin a globe and from that shadow
Create a moon. I imagine its clear
Fullness over Binn Mhór, the touch of frost
That makes you settle deeper in our bed.

Holiday Poem

The cheek of you, leaning out
To open shutters and pour sunlight

Over last night's wine and clothes.
The marsh where yesterday

We gathered sea-lavender and caught
The kingfisher's rainbow darts

Stretches in birdcalls below you
Leaning out, bare-arsed over Brittany.

Night Start

Sleep easy, love, the day will come around
And light the glass, and warm the windowsill.
Lie close, lie still, you only dreamt that sound.

Forget you heard the snarling of the hound,
The harsh breath, the snap that almost killed
Sleep. Easy, love. The day will come around.

That wail is not the voices of the drowned,
But the salt wind beating up the hill.
Lie close, lie still. You only dreamt that sound.

And that was not a tremor of the ground,
Just my arm shivering in a sudden chill.
Sleep easy. Love. The day will come around.

I conjure past and future to surround
This night, this room, to witness that we still
Lie close. Lie still, you only dreamt that sound.

So rest, my love, assured. What we have found
Settles around us, an earnest that we will
Sleep easy. Love, the day will come around.
Lie close. Lie still. We only dreamt that sound.

Tides

Last night the hollow of your back
Was the moon and its shadow curving
One into the other, your kiss
The ripple of tides tonguing the shore
Now and again, now and again.

This morning, as the early light
Swelled and the curtains stirred,
The cadences of the tide flowed
Into your breathing, each breath
Becoming the other, becoming the other.

Seahorses in Dingle

Their serenity, you said, and the slow
Celebratory dance between partners

> Every single morning of their lives
> Had drawn you first to their tank.

Now once again you are watching them
Floating pacifically in the aquarium,

> Uncoiling themselves from weeds to rise
> Dreamily towards their own reflections,

Gliding with stellar detachment
Through shifting planes of light,

> Curling and uncurling into tentative
> Question marks that seek no answers.

For ages, rapt, hardly breathing, your eyes
Reflecting water, light, you watch them probe

> The depths and limits of their glassy space,
> As you, in your element, absorb their grace.

Christmas Shopping List

For my wife I ordered that the sun
Be freshly squeezed each morning of her life,
That the moon ceremoniously attend
On all of her comings and goings
And that the stars should never cease
Doing the rounds of her eyes.

For my daughter I command that roads
Be laid smoothly between mountains,
That rivers echo guidance along valleys,
That a fair wind rise to bring her
In good time again and again to swim
In the morning waves of her childhood.

For my son let the satellites beam
Messages of love precisely here and there
For the time being, and the grids that net
The seas and continents direct him
To all the coordinates he chooses,
Then catch and trawl him home.

And for myself, if all of this
Might come to pass in seven days,
What more could I want? I would know
That I was right to have ideas
Above my station, and I would
Be complete and know that it was good.

19 December 1999

Corra Bána

do Éanna

Bhí sé beagnach dearmadta agam, an crann sin
A chonac ón mbus, taobh amuigh de bhaile,
É breac le corra bána suite mar a bheadh éarlais
Ar ghrástúlacht, fad saoil agus bheith ann don eile.

Fad saoil chugat féin, mar sin, a rug abhaile
Ód chuid taistil féin an bhratóg shíoda,
Deartha leis na héin rathúla chéanna
A thuirling im aigne le cleitearnach aoibhinn.

Agus tá siad neadaithe i gcónaí faram,
Ag saibhriú an tseomra le cumhracht na Síne,
Suite gan bhogadh ar ghiúis is ar charraig.
Is nuair a chraitheann an bhratóg i bpuithín gaoithe,

Cloisim, ar feadh soicind, mionabhar na síoraíochta
Sa leoithne éadrom ag siosarnach trín síoda.

White Cranes

for Éanna

It had almost slipped my mind, that tree
Glimpsed once from a trundling bus,
Dappled with cranes like long-standing promises
Of grace, long life and the truth of otherness.

So long life to you too, for bringing home
From your own travels this painted silk
Bright with those same auspicious birds,
To land in my mind on exhilarated wings.

They are nesting still in my sitting-room wall,
Endowing the room with wealth from the east,
Perched now for good on rocks among pine-trees,
And, when the scroll stirs in a sudden breeze,

I hear for a moment in that passing wind
Murmurs of eternity rustling through the silk.

Midwife

for Ciairín

Daughter, that time you fell
From the high bank, in slow
Motion it seemed,
Your two-year-old body turning
Into the black and white
Suddenly loud Caragh river,
And your wide eyes pleaded for breath
Instead of that liquid burning:
That, indeed, was like a little death.

Daughter, after my stretched hand
Had slipped—hair floating away—
And slipped again, grasped, pulled
You, gasping, from the heaving water,
You cried, you were not hurt,
And you were swaddled up
In someone's coat, while the whole earth
Breathed again: O daughter,
That, indeed, was like another birth.

High Tide

for my mother at 70

When he married a woman from the mountain,
My father says, he married the mountain too.
I trace connections also with rock and cliff,
With the sand whispering always of beginnings,

With the sea above all, singing beyond herself.
I came to this shore storied with her barnacles,
Bright with the lightning of her shoals, bearing
In deep trust the echoes of her whale-song.

The encircling mountains voice her name
To shells contemplating their whorled infinities.
Burnished seaweed offers droplets to the sun
And rockpools delight in the amazement of stars.

From the waves rolling in a high tide,
A susurration of pebbles, murmurings of love.

Words

for my father at 70

Sifting through my store of words, I recall
The discovery of words you dropped
Like hazelnuts in autumn. I played the squirrel.

It was my right, it was 'finders keepers',
And when words passed like storms through woods
The hoard was safe, there were no 'losers weepers'.

Words sang the pale moon over mountains,
Cried over Uncle Tom's black agony,
Groped among the cliffs of Coomasaharn.

They balanced perilously on overhanging branches
And, on a night-time walk for sweets, filled
Our pockets with flavours that lased.

There are words that wait in the shadows
Like kingfishers under bridges. These I offer.

Stroke

I

Stroke. The verb is gentle, whispering
Good news or bad with balanced intent,
The inevitable synonymous with the possible.

The noun's abruptness, on the other hand,
Announces arbitrary decrees, sudden strokes
Of pens, or whips, indifferently dispensed.

They both combined to form your sentence.
How gently you placed your feet when, delicate
As a bird, you dizzily walked the garden!

Even in the ambulance, the hospital,
The gradualness of your stroke at first
Deceived us, softened into a routine

Of gathering for crumbs of reassurance.
For days, for weeks, we scattered or settled,
Brooding over our different hopes

Until the shell of potential cracked
Open, the verb turned to its noun
And stroke became its brutal fact.

II

And how is he now? People would ask.
Day by day it grew more difficult
to answer. The questions seemed to be

Not really about you. Those puppet steps
You took, supported between physios,
Did they measure progress, or calibrate despair?

I remembered the long strides by hedges
When you stepped acres all over,
It seemed, every county in Ireland,

Valuing the land you had mapped out,
Every town, village and mileage spinning
Easily off your tongue. Now we watched you

Struggle to name familiar landmarks
We had passed on our way to visit.
There was no response I could carry home

To phone calls or neighbours who posed
The same unanswerable question. So how
Was he now? Much the same, I supposed.

III

How endless are the vistas of hospitals!
Nurses disappearing down corridors, their laughter
Tinkling into silence. Wheelchairs silently

Moving along identical white passages.
Lifts humming non-stop between floors.
Even lying in your ward demanded

New perspectives. There was your bed and
The next one and the next one while you lay
And tried to understand your tubed and taped

Indignities. How could your battered brain not reel
Before such immensities! Climbers and divers
Who lose their lines and whose elements

Betray them into passages they have not mapped,
In panic or euphoria will grasp and plunge
Towards certainties they've left behind.

And, so it was, you turned your face
To walls that weren't there, and finding
No familiar limits, fell through space.

IV

Why am I in this peculiar postion?
You asked in the physiotherapy gym
When you began a more circumspect

Conversation with your surroundings.
As the daily rotation lost its meaning
Your language grew in obliqueness.

Sometimes it was truer than the words
We hid behind: when I returned
Unexpectedly, to find you crying silently

And asked if it would help to talk,
You shook your head, waved me away.
I'm just bleeding, you said, from my eyes.

And when you raved about fire and danger,
Rambled about guards and prisoners of war,
You spoke the truth much plainer than we dared.

Realities which had escaped were caught,
Transformed. The world for you was image now,
And metaphor the final end of thought.

Jasmine

What colour is jasmine? you asked
Out of the blue from your wheelchair.
And suddenly the ward was filled
With the scent of possibility, hints
Of journeys to strange parts.

The question floored us. But the gulf
Was not the colours that we couldn't name
But that we couldn't recognise the road
Your question had travelled, nor sound the extent
Of the void to which it would return.

The ward remade itself in a hum
Of conscientious care. Outside, the usual
Traffic jams. We took the long way home.
Father, jasmine is a climbing plant
With scented white or yellow flowers.

And may the fragrance of its blossoms twine
Around the broken trellises of your mind.

Birdman

I remember your face, blank as an owl's,
In all that aimless busyness of therapy,
And my frustration, moving towards despair,
As the physio prompted your right hand
To your left shoulder, or the blue star
Into the yellow box, and you fumbled
And tried to wave the whole thing away.

And I remember how your head cocked
When, on a hunch, I showed you the bird-chart,
And how, at my tentative *show me a blackbird,*
Now show me a swallow, your finger rose and circled
And stabbed time after time, as casually accurate
As a sparrow picking at seed, a heron spearing fish,
Or a crow tearing a rabbit crushed by passing wheels.

From a Train

I

It was a bit the worse for wear, that train
That pulled itself laboriously out of Heuston
Towards the west. I tried to read.
Through drifts of fog we trundled slowly

Across the points at Portarlington.
For no reason but that sway and clatter
I remembered how much you loved the train,
The permutations of fields, even in winter.

Suddenly, I could almost hear you
Admonish me to put away my book
And look at what was passing by, the bogs,
The flooded meadows, the silhouetted trees.

II

It always seemed a kind of magic when
You recognised the winter shapes of trees.
I never thought to match those skeletons
With the shape and shine of leaves and nuts

You would spill into my hands, my eyes
Absorbing what I missed of your half-heard
Words of explanation in the Phoenix Park
Or the Sunday afternoon by-roads of Meath.

The winged seeds that helicoptered
Exuberantly away from a sycamore,
The chestnut's candle-buds, its fishbone leaves,
Its burnished conkers bursting from their shells,

Had no need of any larger pattern,
And the shiny cups and grainy saucers
Of acorns clustered among serrated leaves
Were complete in their own repetition.

III

So much later, with you gone, so much
Was suddenly, lurchingly recognisable
When, as the jolting train left miles of track
Behind it across the sodden midlands,

Those bare outlines, unmistakably beech,
Clarified themselves out of the fog,
Lining an avenue that disappeared
Towards some stately home or another.

And as their newly familiar shapes
Receded into the distance, I recalled
How two parallel lines can never meet,
Except, perhaps, in their infinity.

Geit Áthais

Is ní féidir liom fós tiomáint thar abhainn
In Áth Dara, gan *Slán Le Máighe*
A chloisint á ardú go cúthaileach agat,
Mar gurbh iad caor, craobh agus cuach
Ba dhual i gcónaí duit agus dúchas
Seachas loime agus faobhracht na farraige
A thaobhaíos féin níos minice.

Agus fós tar éis seacht mbliain, iompaím
Le geit iontais seabhac a fheiscint
Croctha gan bogadh os cionn faille,
Na gloiní íslithe agam od lorg
Chun creathadh ar éigin sin na sciathán
A rianú agus a roinnt leat.

Agus go leor eile: an fál nua ag tabhairt fothaine,
Na bláthanna móinéir ag fás go rábach anois,
Teacht is imeacht páistí, tráchtas a scríobhas,
Dánta a foilsíodh, leabhair le foilsiú,
Clingireacht na dtréad cois locha sa tSlóibhéin,
An solas ag sileadh trín duilliúr ar an sliabh.

Agus éist! Tá rón ag ceol amuigh ar Charraig Éanna.
Ach táir gluaiste intíre, i bhfad siar thar abhainn.

"Surprised by Joy ..."

Even still I cannot cross the river
In Adare, without hearing you
Break diffidently into Slán le Maighe,
Because it was berry, branch and cuckoo
That were ever in your blood and breeding
More than the sharp and bare-edged sea.

And even after seven years I turn
With sudden wonder on seeing a hawk
Hanging motionless above a cliff,
Lowering the binoculars to look for you
To delineate and to share
The just-about-trembling of those wings.

And much more: the shelter of the new hedge,
The meadow flower seed I scattered,
The kids' comings and goings, a dissertation,
Poems published, books to come,
The tinkle of cattle-bells in Slovenia
And sunlight through foliage on the mountain.

And listen! A seal is quavering on Carraig Éanna.
But you have moved inland, far across the river.

Bolus

i.m. Máire Uí Chinnseala

At Bolus, where on a pet day we parked
At the end of the road, high over the sea,
You sat out in a folding chair, you the walker,

Who in your health had never bothered with drives
Or views, or nuisances like the binoculars
You now focused on distant islands. And then:

Well, this is just paradise! I flinched away,
Hearing your words beat their huge black wings
Against the fragile day. But when I turned

Your wasting face was radiantly matter-of-fact
And that cacophonous irony I'd heard
Was echoing only inside my humbled mind.

I remake that day now, and see it plain,
Rinsed clear of all ironies, see you
Fold up your chair and walk, into wholeness.

Skellig Cycle

DAWN

Was stone at first with no escape
From the oppression of cells. Outside
Light struggled to penetrate

The hard slate of sea and rock
And failed to find the relief
Carvings on the high cross

Whose arms stretched wide and black
Over the shapeless and eroded
Gravestone of every anonymous monk.

Light at last became a horizon.
The sun began its definitions
And the night shapes of the island

Softened themselves into morning.
Voices and the beating of wings
Became birds, were simply dawnsong

Up and down where cliffs unfurled
Each layer to where the waves again
Broke on the shores of this world.

MORNING

Saw mackerel in a silver zigzag
Drawn by a quivering line
Below the monk's steps, flashing

149

From darkness like souls drawn
To God. Slit, gutted, washed,
They earned an hour's sprawl

In the sun, before six hundred steps
Trudged again their dogged path
To the hunched and remote cells.

In the sunlight, archaeologists
Surveyed the enclosure, probing
The inarticulate past for promises

Of revelations. Their squared paper
And standard record sheets absorbed
The details as they patiently

Measured the width at base, height
And average depth of each cell
Doorway retreating from the light.

NOON

Drew heat from stone, carried
The eye up and down crevices
Where clumps of seapink balanced

Between water and sky. Haze
Dissolved the horizon until only
The island perspective remained,

Stonily insistent on the vertical.
To walk with levelled mainland eyes
Was to stumble. Here was the subversion

150

Of all the horizontals of the mind
And time and space. The day
Found the present undermined

And wavered between the past
And the unknown. Knowledge
Measured its incapacity to grasp

Even the questions of the island.
The sun stared straight down,
Impassively judging the silence.

EVENING

Drew shadows along ledges
Where rabbits snatched intervals
Of grazing from the kestrel

Circling in the sun's last rays.
There was time to run a finger
Along a grooved cross, to praise

The skilled hermit hands
Chipping slivers of himself
Into the score of the island's

Canticle of worship. His cave
Renounced the small companionship
Of the enclosure, and craved

The wind skinning the backbone
Of the island. It was time
For tins and gas-stoves,

Sliced loaves and mackerel, a walk
To the lighthouse for keepers' stories
And, on TV news, the world's small talk.

NIGHT

Brought sleeping bags and torches
Flickering up steps and ledges
Grown prodigious in the darkness.

The lighthouse beam swept above
A pause for breath on Christ's saddle.
Wind rose abysmally from the cove

Pitch black below. God muttered
Among rocks where Christ existed
Only in name. Wings bursting

In confusion through torchbeams
Were laughed away, but nonetheless
Seemed visitations from a dream

Not fully woken from. Boulders
Swollen by shadows of themselves
Formed an escort to the enclosure.

In the beehive cells, stone
Floors and walls barely reflected
Candlelight fitfully until dawn.

South Peak Hermitage, Skellig

Questions become my certainties
Each day on the bare peak
Scaling hand over hand
Over foothold to God.

What is this sheer rock
Plunging and rising
To and from the abyss?
Upon this rock I will build.

What is the air's true voice?
Gales lash my oratory, but seabirds
Land gently on warm wings.
There are many voices.

Where is the fire on the rock?
In the soul's forging, hammered
Bright to outlast the flames
That burn the untempered soul.

What is the surrounding water?
In the soft-noted woods
We coveted chastening deserts.
This is my salty waste.

In the name of the Father, hidden
In clouded skies, of the water
Flowing in the baptism of the Son,
And of the fire of the Holy Spirit,

I will cling to this hard rock
Until I become no more
And no less than a syllable
In the breath of the Word.

Ceallúnach

These blank and scattered
Headstones spell out
A gospel of rejection.
Here among the vestiges

Of an early monastery
Numbed hands gleaned comfort
In gathering the stones
Of a crumbling oratory

To mark the graves
Of infants, dead without
The words and incense
And sprinkling of salvation.

This was their limbo,
A furtive alliance
With suicides and the odd
Drowned, dark sailor

Against whom the Fathers,
Sitting in gravest council,
Locked the huge gates
Of their high, new Church.

It should now be known
Among these outcast bones
That this ceallúnach
Is just an anachronism,

Because the robed men,
Gathering again in conclave,
Pronounced that their Church
Had changed her mind.

Yet here still, Fathers,
Read the stone letters,
Although your hard words
Were written on water!

Digging

Remembering from the beginning
That digging will discover nothing
Unless the ground has first
Been probed in the imagination,

Sink yourself deep into it,
Absorbing seed and pollen,
The insinuations of clay.
Below the tangle of roots,

Be alert for voices,
A hint of ashes or smoke,
The stench of midden
And, always, the hammering of stone.

Follow the incense of ceremony,
A strain of bone flutes.
Be yourself companion to
Bodysmells of fear, and love.

Only then open your eyes
And mark out your site
With appropriate measurements
Methodically, square by square.

Extract and piece together
The random shards you had sensed.
There will be a tentative, half glimpsed
Outline of bowl or amphora

Whose fragments and splinters,
Aching for vanished completeness,
Can fuse into something
Discovering the shape of itself.

Cill Rialaig

At Cill Rialaig, high
On the bare headland,
The wind is skinning
The side of the mountain.

You can almost see it
Peeling the thin soil,
Heather and furze
Down to the bare rock,

As the monks once peeled
The world from their lives
And shed their selves
In search of another.

From these high ruins
The waves seem flattened.
Occasional shafts of light
Silver the ocean

So that it gleams
Like a bell, or a chalice
Which the clouds chase
With patterns of praise.

On this hard slope
Everything is edge.
The rough stone of cells
Is poor enough shelter.

To exorcise the wind
Here you must raise
Chalice and bell, huddle
Around book and candle.

Cross Slab, Church Island

A vertically disposed inscription commences on
the shaft of the cross and continues on its dexter side.
—Archaeologist's Report

In the Annals of Inisfallen
He was *God's anchorite.*
On the island, his inscription
Is simpler in stone.

Beannacht for anmain Anmchada
The slab implores.
But the blessing on his soul
(The sculptor misjudging space)

Edged 'Anmchada' off the shaft,
To rest like a tender afterthought
Tucked, almost embraced,
Between the arm and body of the cross.

God's anchorite hugged by God,
Helpmate in the eternal
Protection of God's right arm.
My boat rocks in small waves.

If I open the newspaper
With the picnic in the boat
There will be familiar stories
From north and east

Of killings and cleansings
In the name of one
Group or another for
Or against some cross.

A blessing indeed on Anmchad
Whose island never discovered,
In inquisitions or holy wars,
The sinister side of God.

Fiddler, Church Island

The harmony of the small
Ruined church remains
Like deconstructed musical
Instruments in paintings.

Its east to west axis
Becomes an airy string
Played from the altar window
To the Romanesque doorway.

Between the roofless nave
And chancel, the imagined
Mediation of an arch
Rests on its broken pillars

Where carved sitting snug
(Always one who'll refuse to go!)
A stone fiddler is playing
Away by the new time.

God know his friends
And relations probably spread
Themselves over the arch,
Making for an almighty session.

Blank-faced, intent on music,
He has for centuries
Repeated his noble call
To make the stone sing.

His music is the constant
Plainsong of water
Graced by matins, lauds
And nones of larks.

Lohar

for Father Gorazd Vopatrny

Alpha and Omega
Are carved hanging
From the arms of the cross
On the stone slab at Lohar.

I never showed this
To the Russian orthodox monk
Who prayed there, rapt.
I was still wondering

How an incredulous boatman,
Against all good judgement,
Had ferried him that day
Through a storm to Skellig.

It was simply, he smiled,
A *peregrinatio pro Christi:*
He could not go home
Without praying on the island.

He bent to kiss
And stroke the cross,
Long robes flapping
Like a windblown crow.

Then, with the realisation
That Skellig and its cells
Lay just beyond the headland,
He turned towards the sea,

His whole bearing
An infusion of love,
And carved a blessing
Deep into the wind.

My prayer is that seabirds
Winged his benediction
Straight to the be all
And end all of his journey.

Gable Shrine, Killoluaig

Give me my scallop shell of quiet,
My staff of faith to walk upon.
—Walter Ralegh, *'The Pilgrim'*

In the gable shrine,
Its end-piece dislodged,
You can see the gleaming
Of propitious quartz

Among the discoloured fragments
Of sanctified bones.
Yet what startles the eye
Into searching for wonders

Are the scallop shells,
Their fluted and serrated
Shapes frayed and cracked
Yet elegant between the stones,

As if Venus might rise
Tentatively from the sea,
Floating towards rebirth
On a lacework of foam.

Aroint thee! It was sterner
Visions brought these shells
Here to these bare slabs
In continous devotion, echoing

The emblem of pilgrims
To Santiago de Compostela,
Borne in triumphant penitence
Along the roads of Europe.

Now this votive cache
Lies among nameless bones,
Its currency of veneration
Long since devalued.

Here the world is a shell,
Empty and unhinged,
Bleached to an inarticulate
Dreaming of tongues.

An Géarchaoineadh, Sceilg Mhichíl

do Mhícheál Ua Ciarmhaic

Bean An Uaill a luaitear liom go minic. N'fheadar.
Táim chomh fada sin cromtha im charraig
Ná cuimhin liom bheith baineann ná fireann,
Ná feadar an caointeoireacht fir nó caointeoireacht mná
A bhíonn anois agam, nó a bhí ariamh agam …
Caointeoireacht cloiche, seachas aon rud eile.
Seachtarach do gach aon rud eile. Scoite.

Táim ag caoineadh réabadh na carraige,
An chloch chruaidh scoiltithe uaithi féin,
Na leaca a leagadh ina gcéimeanna,
Á gcasúiriú chun cruiceogachta, á smachtú
Ag clingireacht clog, ag crónán paidreacha.
Táim ag caoineadh na carraige ina smionagar
Ag púdar buile innealltóirí, failltreacha
Brúite, briste chun bóthair, chun tí solais.
Táim ag caoineadh mo dhíothú féin,
Mé athmhúnluithe ag oilithrigh is ag aimsir.

Tá mo dhá lámh sínte romham amach
Agus uaireanta tagann éanacha chugam,
Ag déanamh, mar dhea, neamhshuim díom
Is de mo dhúire, a súile is a gclúmh
Ar bís chun aeir agus chun solais.
Ach tagann siad fós ag tuirlingt orm
Faoi mar ba naomh mé i seanscéal,
Mar a bheidís faoi gheasa ag mo chaoineadh.

/…

166

Wailing Woman, Skellig Michael

The Wailing Woman, they mostly call me. I don't know.
I am so long bent over into stone
That I don't remember being man or woman,
I don't know if it's a man's keening or a woman's
I make now, or ever made ...
A rock's keening, more than anything else.
External to everything else. Alien.

I wail for the rupturing of the rock,
The adamant rock splintered from itself,
The slabs being set into steps,
Hammered into beehive huts, dominated
By tinkling bells, the drone of prayer.
I mourn the rock in smithereens
By the mad powder of engineers, cliffs
Battered and bruised into a road, a lighthouse.
I am wailing for my own uprooting,
My transformation by pilgrims and the weather.

My hands are spread out before me
And sometimes birds come to me,
Pretending to ignore me,
Ignore my hardness, their eyes and plumage
Eager for air and for light.
But they still come to land on me,
As if I were a sainted legend,
As if they're in thrall to my wailing.

/...

Tá Críost a chaoineadh agam, mar adeir siad,
In éineacht le mná caointe Iérúsaileim.
Ach táim ag caoineadh freisin na mná caointe
Ar fad, thoir, thiar, thuaidh agus theas,
Lámh spréite acu chun cheamara, lámh eile
Ag dáileadh bratacha ar ógánaigh.
Táim ag caoineadh na gcaointeoirí
Is iad ag ceiliúradh na caointeoireachta abú.

Táim ag caoineadh glúinte gonta na noilithreach
A ghabh tharam ag siosarnach píonóis.
Táim ag caoineadh mo bhodhaire féin dá bpaidreacha,
Is a mbodhaire siúd do hósanna an aeir ina dtimpeall.

Táim cromtha faoi ualach na gealaí,
Faoina reoiteacht; faoina séanadh
Mí i ndiaidh míosa, rabharta i ndiadh rabharta,
Gurb í mo mháthair í agus máthair na farraige,
Gurb í tuile agus trá, dá hainneoin féin.

Ach umhlaím gach maidin roimh ghealadh an lae
Anoir chugam ón mhórthír, mo dhrom
Go diongabháilte le dul faoi na gréine,
Mar gur mó liom soineantacht an tsolais ar maidin
Ná ciall cheannaigh an dorchadais i ndeireadh an lae.
Agus coinneod m'aghaidh mar fhuinneog altóra
Chun an oirthir, ag súil le fuipíní áiféiseacha
Ag filleadh arís is arís le gobanna ioldaite lán éisc.

I wail for Christ, as is rightly said,
With the wailing women of Jerusalem.
But I wail also for the wailing women
Everywhere, east, west, north and south,
One arm spread to the camera, the other
Distributing flags to the young.
I mourn for the mourners
Who celebrate the mourning.

I mourn for the raw knees of pilgrims
Who pass me by whispering punishment,
I mourn my deafness to their prayers
And their deafness to the hosanna of the surrounding air.

I am bent under the weight of the moon,
Her iciness; of her denial,
Month after month, tide after spring tide,
That she is my mother and the sea's mother,
That she is, despite herself, the flow and the ebb.

But I bow each morning before the dawn
Rising to me from the mainland, my back
Resolutely to the setting sun,
For I value the innocence of morning light
More than the dearly bought knowledge of evening darkness.
And I will keep my face like an altar window
To the east, waiting for ludicrous puffins to return
Again and again with multicoloured, fish-brimming beaks.

Holy Well, Coad

Roads once crisscrossed the mountain,
Carting butter to Cork,
Jolting copper ore from the mines
Down to the small harbour.

The open well mirrors
A shimmer of sky and mountain
Holding deep below the surface
The memory of the many

Pilgrims constantly deepening
With a small, sharp stone
The grooves of the simple
Christ's cross on the slab.

The round of three wells
Was a blessing in common,
A balm for failing sight
Or older fears of the dark.

The holy tree, its branches
Leaved with rags, and coins
Pressed into its flesh,
Is a splinter in the memory.

Only the path remains,
Guiding us from well to well,
The movement always
Clockwise in propitiation.

Secular pilgrims with rucksacks,
We expect no miracles. It's enough
To return with eyes rinsed
Clean for the daily round.

Skellig

COMBAT

Nothing in Europe is farther west. Pitched
Seven miles past the uttermost headlands
Two cones of fissile rock settle. The sea
Swallows the strain of the earth's bones creaking.
Here Michael the hermit clawed with the Devil
And, in a time of absolutes, wrestled him
From the high crags, flung him in the tide
To slink with other monsters. Battered, bitter
He soured the water around Cornwall too.
But in high Mont Saint-Michel, gilded Michael
With a blessed engraved blade broke him,
Banished him formally to the long Normandy tides.
    That Easter, in ten thousand churches,
Ten thousand clergy chanted *Lumen Christi*,
Challenging darkness with their Paschal candles,
And all of Europe thundered *Deo Gratias*.

GOTHIC

It's different at Mont Saint-Michel, causewayed
And chronicled through the tides of history;
Each airy layer illuminating sainthood,
All light and order, buttressing belief.
    Skellig makes its own Gothic. Spires
Of lichened slate thrust upwards
Over arched caves and parapets
Gargoyled with bizarre rows of guillemots.
In cliffsides dark against the rose-window

Of sunset, stony niches are statued with gulls;
While below the island's cloistered paths
The huge sea-polished slabs are washed
And choired with the plain chant of seals.

DAY TRIP

It's always a difficult landing. A bad draw
In the small cove sends the boat lurching
Awkwardly to the pier, as if the sea
Is uneasy, reluctant to disclaim possession.
Slowly the island takes hold, steadies
The visitor, discovers its paths again.
Up steps no longer penitential, bright-shirted
We straggle towards the top. Through the lucent
Surrounding air, gannets like angels circle
And plunge and rise again and again.
Below, kittiwakes shriek like the damned.
Facile allegories flutter on all sides:
Puffins like gaudy cardinals pose
Defiantly, exotics from another climate.
Horizons, nonetheless, seem to expand
Towards dissolution, abjuring earthbound communion.
    There are mindfalls among these cliffs
Where through dark nights souls hung waiting
For the light, traversing awful ledges.
We live on lower ground. High things subdued
By time and absence fascinate
Without terror. With sunlight spilt on the rocks
There is no *dies irae*, no fear in tenebrous cells.
These stone beehive huts once droned morning
Noon and night prayers, disciplined by bells,
Regular and momentous as the tides. Today

Storm petrels gurgle warmly in the crevices
Amidst the click and buzz of automatic Pentaxes.

MISSION

Skellig. A sliver of sound to penetrate
The silence of our new millennium.
Apocalypse a thousand years ago erupted
From Viking longboats onto Skellig.
Small entries in the annals formalise
The terror that eclipsed those tonsured heads,
The spilled hosts, the clang of chalices on rock.
    Around Skellig now the long boats are silent
Under pewter seas. Humming screens
Quietly formalise our new apocalypse.
In Holy Loch to the North, exiled monks
Based their mission *ad majorem Dei gloriam.*
Now from their base at Holy Loch, nuclear
Submarines in seal grey slip from the shore
On missions towards God knows what.
    Silent like sharks, but echoing
Internally a blasphemy of whalesong,
They glide towards mapped manoeuvres
South of Skellig. *In hoc signo vinces.*

WAITING

The visitors have gone. The lighthouse, now unmanned,
Sends its automatic beam for miles above the water.
Below the soft swell of the great lunar heaves
Around Skellig, all the long boats of Europe wait,
Their sights fixed on the high, unsainted peaks.

VI

Wren

The whirr of trapped panicky wings, a small
Thump, then silence. When I found you lying
In a double-glazed stupor near the window
And held you in my cupped hands, little king

Of all birds I thought you'd never live
Until Stephen's Day to be caught in the furze.
To cover you and keep you warm was just
A kindness towards your quivering frailty.

So when, again unseen, you pushed aside
Your winding–sheet and whirred straight out
The open door, it was like found money
To hurry to the window and to see you.

Tail cocked, strutting your tiny stuff
In and out of crevices in a wall,
Exploring pockets of light and air
Between the weight and darkness of the stones.

And when you climbed the ladder of seed-pods
To sway and sing in the ruffling wind,
My heart sang too, as if suddenly lifted
To majestic heights on an eagle's back.

January Epiphanies

Snow being rare here, I walked out early,
Hoping to concelebrate sunrise with music.
Rushes and furze stood stiff with amazement
And sallies experimented with the new weight

On their branches. Light tingled across fields
And crystals here and there sparkled an answer
Like an orchestra tuning up. As the sun cleared
The mountain behind me, it was almost dancing.

I had brought Sibelius for the Walkman,
So the sun became percussion and *Finlandia* boomed
Across the whole epic mile of snowy waste
Back to my house. I put the kettle on and hummed

The tune we sang in the pub last night, the one
Where the thrush and the robin their sweet notes entwine,
And when I pulled the curtains to check the bird-table,
My mind somewhere between Lapland and Mooncoin,

A ruffle-feathered thrush was chasing a robin
Away from its share of the breadcrumbs and seeds.
They weren't entwining their sweet notes; but still,
Still, today is the Feast of the Epiphany.

Lapse at Innisfallen

Wild roses through the Romanesque
Altar-window overlooking the lake
Distract the celebrant at Innisfallen.

His hands falter over the bread and wine.
Despite himself, they bless instead the roses
As he murmurs *Body*, whispers *Blood*.

Later, for a penance, he will copy out
For the umpteenth time, and then erase,
Year after year of the monastery's annals

That chronologise, in perfect script,
Pillagings, successions, the consecration
Of abbots and the violent deaths of kings.

Guide Dog

for Mollie Coffey

I'm only scribbling in the shadows now,
You wrote, asking for a poem
About the Inny Strand, once better

Than a whole world of tranquillisers,
But beyond you now, you said,
Unless you get a guide dog.

So here's this guide dog, scratching
At the backdoor of your memory.
Just wrap yourself in something warm

And let yourself out. Whisper your own
Private commands and he'll bring you
Easily through the fields to the strand

Dreaming in spring moonlight, or washed
Clean and hard by winter tides.
On limpid June days you'll see

Men in seine-boats, shoulders tensed
For the salmon's splash that'll send
The oars straining to circle the shoal.

If it's warm and the tide is low
You can walk across the ferry,
Carrying your shoes in your hand.

And while you sit down to watch the swell
Breaking over Carraig Éanna or The Blue Boys
And recall a verse of *Mo Shlán Beo Soir*,

Your dog will walk through pools of reflection,
Leaving long trails of pawmarks
Across huge skies and passing clouds.

He'll chase seagulls that have settled
Stiffly in rows along the tide-line
Like forgotten years, scattering them

Into urgencies of strident protest
At his delirious barking and abandoned
Spray-scattering race through the waves.

And when he brings you home again
And scratches at the door, let yourself
Back in and put the kettle on the range.

Yangshuo River Walk

for Qin Jiang Rong

My rolls of film, now developed, scroll
Down that drizzling day again, the river
Unwinding itself between pinnacles
Draped exquisitely over themselves.

Bamboos drooping with mist crisscross
As we crisscrossed the river between villages
Dirt poor among rich orchards, rice paddies
And *sweet potatoes only for the festival.*

Once again I am being ink-brushed
Into a landscape more insubstantial
Than the mist where it is cocooned.
I am complicit in my own disappearance.

But the mud of that river walk clings
In my memory as it clung to my boots,
And I still taste the pomelo whose seeds
We spat in circles of laughter around us,

As the cruise-boats on the river klaxoned,
And you recited Li Bai, so that I heard
For the first time the pattern and rhyme
Of his loneliness and moonlit exile.

I put the photographs away in the drawer
Of my imagination. The gloss changes,
Begins to spin itself into a silk scroll,
Unwinding as my pen becomes a brush.

Planting Garlic

I

The tenth of January, I must be mad,
My neighbour says, as I prepare the ground.
But the gleam on pike after sunlit

Pikeful of seaweed belies the season,
Foresees the spring in the sodden earth
That clings in black lumps to my boots.

I mark my ridge, the spade awkward
In the sticky clay, then shovel up
From the furrow. The dark rectangle

Shapes itself slowly over the seaweed.
Now it will be drying, silently coaxing
The rich fronds towards their sweet decay.

II

I prise open a bulb, my fingers
All at once releasing hints of sap
Like a memory in the frosty air.

The separated cloves look fit to burst
With newness, gleaming on the clay
Like stars that have dropped to earth.

Here, spread out, are feasts to come,
With mussels opening in anticipation,
Tomatoes and herbs racing to the smell!

And there will be the conjuring of summer
When the door of the shed creaks open
On plaited sunshine stored in airy bunches.

III

And may there be no need for any cures,
No catch in the breath to be eased by infusions
Or a clove in red flannel around the neck,

Nor for a clove to be anxiously pressed
Into the shoes of children, to ward off
The hectic red cheeks of consumption,

Nor yet for the clove stitched tight
Into the tails of cattle, to purify
Blood and water against the black disease.

Now is my time for a cleansing of the blood,
Here, in this garden, this day and all
This magic is a cure beyond belief.

IV

Two inches deep, six inches apart,
The cloves pattern the soil. I repeat
The instructions like a mantra as I plant.

I sniff at the pungency that's charm
Against werewolves and vampires,
And I place my cloves in exorcism

Of all the darkness I fear within
And without myself, and of all seasons
That would suck the light from the world.

And so to mark the limits of my patch
I drive a stake down into the ridge
And straight through the heart of winter.

To Plant Early Potatoes

for Pearse Hutchinson

First pike your manure three feet wide
Across the length your ridge will be,
Wallowing in the frenzy of feeding
And copulating dung-flies this releases.
(It must be some other kind of fly
Those swallows crisscrossing the sky
Are taking by the dozen on the wing).

The sods you mark, and lift, and fold
Flat on their backs on the ridge
Will start a furrow on either side
To take the water. This is also
Where you will bury the fresh stalks
Of the earliest potatoes you dig
Lest they blight the rest of the crop.

Now you must split the turned sods
Wide open with your spade. Do not
Allow your neighbours hear you talk
Of wandering playboys who might cleave
A skull, or you could be locked away.
Half-baked invocations of poets with earthy
Ulster accents should likewise be kept to yourself.

Take your seed that have been sprouted
Softly in the dark before being hardened
By the experience of light, and place them
In the clefts that you made in the sods.
Another row will marble the centre of the ridge.

Invite the robin, who has hopped closer
And ever closer, to observe the pattern.

Now from your furrow shovel the earth
In a neat, dark rectangle over your seed,
And let no graven image cross your mind,
Just the summer's earliest crop tumbling
Exuberantly from the ridge. Finish the job
To admiring—if faintly mocking—whistles, as
Overhead, a flight of curlews catches the light.

Ballyheigue Revisited

Heartyheads we called them, and you lay
Prone beside a rockpool to fish them,
Dangling a bent, barbless pin on a thread,
A piece of leathery *báirneach* for your bait.

First the transparent shrimp in sudden darts
Came gathering around the bait, their little
Tentative nosings vibrating up the thread.
Electric shockers, we said, in tingling delight.

But they were nothing to the heartyhead
That glided out from underneath a ledge,
Brushing aside seaweed and anemones,
Opening his fat mouth towards the bait.

And then you pulled, and almost always
He slipped off the pin. But now and again
You tugged him free of the pool and you stood
And whirled him round, scattering water

In triumphant, sunlit wheels, racing
Impossible distances across the sky
Until you slowed gradually, and anxious
To begin again you knelt and let him go.

More than thirty years later, as I picked
My steps over the same textures of rock,
The ribbed ones that were hard to walk, the smooth
Purple ones that held the heat of the sun,

He took my breath away, that boy—
Intent over the pool, the same
Red curls I once longed to grow out of—
Who looked at me incuriously for a moment

While something barbed and unimaginable
Tugged, and I was rooted to the spot.

Paidir Oíche

do Shiobhán Ní Fhoghlú

Gabhaim buíochas as an lá míorúilteach seo atáim díreach tar éis a
    chaitheamh
Mar ar maidin chuas ag rith ar an dtrá (ag m'aois-se) agus d'éirigh
    liom,
Cé go rabhas mall, rith tríd na scamaill—na scáileanna tá's agat a
    chíonn tú
Ar an ngaineamh fliuch díreach ar imeall na taoide—agus níor
    thiteas.

Agus dheineas anraith, go leor don lá inniu agus cion ceithre lá eile
    sa reoiteoir,
Agus thirimíos dhá líne níocháin, agus i measc cleitearnach agus
    slapar
Na mbraitlíní rith línte anseo is ansiúd liom agus scríobhas agus
    chlóscríobhas
An dán tráthnóna—ní hé an ceann seo é—agus táim sásta leis, is
    dóigh liom.

Agus anois díreach sa choimheascar chualas don gcéad uair i
    mbliana an chuach
Agus cé gurbh im chluais chlé ar mhí-ámharaí an tsaoil a chuala í,
    do chasas
Deiseal ar an dtoirt (agus ar ámharaí an tsaoil) agus tríd is tríd táim
    meáite
Go mbeidh rath ar an mbliain agus ormsa agus ar ghach aon neach
    faoin spéir.

Evening Prayer

for Siobhán Ní Fhoghlú

I give thanks for this miraculous day I have just spent
Because this morning (at my age) I ran on the beach and I managed,
Although I was slow, to run through the clouds—the reflections,
    that is, you see
On the wet sand right at the tide's edge—and I didn't collapse.

And I made soup, enough for today and four more days in the
    freezer,
And I dried two lines of washing, and between the flapping and
    slapping
Of the sheets, some stray lines ran through my head and I wrote
    and typed
The poem this evening—it wasn't this one—and I'm happy with it,
    I think.

And just now in the twilight I heard my first cuckoo this year
And although I heard it inauspiciously in my left ear, I turned
Immediately (and auspiciously) clockwise and overall I am
    determined
That good fortune will attend the year and myself and all creatures
    under the sun.

Ag Aistriú 'Buddha In Der Glorie'

In aghaidh mo thola, bhí sé caite uaim agam,
An smaoineamh go n-aistreoinn an dán sin le Rilke,
Cé go raibh sé fillte agus aithfhillte trím aigne
Mar a bheadh bratóg urnaithe ar chrann naofa.

Fuaireas róchoimhthíoch iad, na críocha úd
Ina raibh dán agus aistriúchán ag taisteal,
An ghramadach débhríoch, agus nósmhaireacht an táirsigh
Suite ar faire roimh mo chead isteach.

Ach nuair a bhaineas mo bhróga iartharacha díom
Roimh gabháil thar táirseach Teampall Phrah Singh,
Is nuair a shuíos croschosach ag análú tiúise,
Cloigíní ag bualadh i leoithne anseo is ansiúd,

D'aithníos Búda Rilke os mo chomhair in airde,
Ceannbhrat naoi gciseal go caithréimeach
Ar foluain os a chionn. I loinnir an íomhá,
Thuigeas go bhféadfaí go ndéanfaí teanga díom.

Translating 'Buddha In Der Glorie'

Against my will, I had put to one side
The notion of translating that poem by Rilke,
Although it had wound itself around my mind
Like a prayer-flag around a holy tree.

They were too alien to me, those regions
Where poem and translation were travelling;
The grammar ambiguous, and the threshold customs
Squatting like guardians against my entering.

But when I took off my Western shoes
Before crossing the threshold of Wat Phrah Singh,
And when I sat, cross-legged, breathing incense,
Temple bells tinkling somewhere in the breeze,

I recognised Rilke's Buddha high up before me,
A nine-tiered canopy floating triumphantly
Above his head. In that resplendent image
I could see the gleam of the gift of tongues.

Búda Faoi Ghlóir

Croí gach chroí, lár gach láir,
Cnó laistigh de féin ag milsiú,
Cruinne na réalt is sia ar fad siar
Is ea toradh d'ioncholluithe: soraidh chugat.

Féach anois nach bhfuil ceangal ort feasta;
Síneann do bhlaosc go dtí críocha na síoraíochta,
Mar a bhfuil an sú láidir ag brúchtaíl in airde.
Tagann loinnir ón dtaobh amuigh á ghríosadh,

Is anois beidh na grianta ar fad os do chionn
Ar dearglasadh, ar chúl a gcinn.
Ach laistigh díot féin tá dúil ag borradh
A mhairfidh tar éis grianta a bheith marbh id dhiaidh.

ó Ghearmáinis Rainer Maria Rilke

Buddha in Glory

Kernel of kernels, core of all cores,
An almond, self-contained and sweetening—
This universe, to the uttermost star,
Is your fruit and flesh: I send you greetings.

Now you know you are unencumbered;
Your shell has stretched into the infinite,
Where the vibrant sap rises and pulses.
An enabling light beams from a distance,

And now all of your suns will revolve,
Rich and glowing high overhead.
But something in you has begun to evolve
That will live when all those suns are dead.

from the German of Rainer Maria Rilke

Ag Éisteacht le Dord na nDamh

do Frank Lewis

Tá an ghrian ag suirí leis an ngeimhreadh sa ghleann
Agus glór ag teacht anall is abhus ar an aer,
Dord mór-is-fiú ag sní ó bheann go beann.

Idir sinn agus léas, faobhrach mar lann,
Féach an damh seacht mbeann greanta ar an spéir.
Tá an ghrian ag suirí leis an ngeimhreadh sa ghleann.

Éist bodhrán an dúlra á bhualadh le fonn,
Píobaireacht na n-éan ag freagairt dá réir
Agus dord mór-is-fiú ag sní ó bheann go beann.

Maireann dord sleá na Féinne i gcuimhne na gcrann
Atá rábach le duilliúr, le cnó is le caor.
Tá an ghrian ag suirí leis an ngeimhreadh sa ghleann.

An ceol is ceolmhaire amuigh, sin ceol gach ní atá ann.
Tá bithnóta ceoil anois á sheinm inár ngaobhar
Agus dord mór-is-fiú ag sní ó bheann go beann.

Tá an glór seo le cianta i scéal agus rann,
Is má chailltear an macalla, díolfar as go daor.
Tá an ghrian ag suirí leis an ngeimhreadh sa ghleann,
Agus dord mór-is-fiú ag sní ó bheann go beann.

Cill Áirne, Deireadh Fómhair 2003

Listening to the Roaring of the Stags

for Frank Lewis

The sun is making love to winter in the glen
And a calling can be heard as it echoes here and there,
An imperious ululation that rolls from ben to ben.

Between us and the light, sharp as a blade's edge,
See the seven-horned stag, etched deep into the air.
The sun is making love to the winter in the glen.

The elemental bodhrán grows more and more intense
As the piping of the birds becomes antiphonal prayer,
And an imperious ululation rolls from ben to ben.

The spear-wail of the Fianna lives on in branch and stem
With leaf and nut and berry in rampant display,
While the sun is making love to the winter in the glen.

The music of what happens is music without end
And a universal note now permeates the air,
An imperious ululation that rolls from ben to ben.

This voice has called through ages in story and in verse
And if we lose its echo, the loss will cost us dear.
The sun is making love to winter in the glen
And an imperious ululation rolls from ben to ben.

Killarney, October 2003

Blasket Roof

for Maria Simonds-Gooding

Of course it was just practical,
Common sense and craft dismantling
An island roof for evacuation
And resettlement on mainland stone.
Driftwood once again, briefly across the sound,
Before that same craft and sense hammered
Its truss-beams cleanly across each other,
It carried nothing now but its own
Weight and proof of freshly tarred felt.

But that same tarred felt would have shone
Like a seal's hide, and I can see too
A roof that sailed across on the wind
Like a tune taken from another world;
Or a boat in a strange landing-place,
Beached above high tide then turned
And tied down to last the winter;
Or even an oratory, safe, dry and echoing,
And crafted to last until God knows when.

Oystercatchers on Uist

for Séamus Ó Catháin

In Uist the oyster-catcher is called 'Brídein', bird of Bríde
—Carmina Gadelica

When I read that, I could see
The long miles of sand, and the birds
In a black and white fuss of scurrying
And dibbling between the *machair* flowers.

Then—maybe I disturbed them—all
At once, as if a bell had sounded,
There was a great flurry of wings
And they were off, wheeling and cheeping

And cheeping and wheeling until it all
Gathered into one limpid consonance.
I could imagine a settlement of sisterhood
Delighted into dancing, in circles widening

And widening forever, and forever singing
Bríd, Bríd, under a great blue cloak of sky.

Ceangailte

Tá an ceo ina shrathar fhada
Ag luascadh ar dhá thaobh
Drom an Bhlascaoid.

Beag beann ar ár leithéidí
Tá an t-oileán ag treabhadh leis
Ag iompar ualach na farraige.

Harnessed

The mist hangs and sways
Like turf-creels on either side
Of the Blasket's backbone.

Oblivious of the likes of us
The island ploughs on
Bearing the load of the sea.

An Logainmneoir

do Bhreandán Ó Cíobháin

Stopann sé scathaimhín ag Carraig Coiscéim,
Ag meá rithim an uisce a scéitheann isteach
Agus amach de réir rúibricí na haimsire.

N'fheadar sé an guth na n-áitreabhóirí
Nó foghar na toinne, nó seanchas ar foluain
Fós ar an ngaoth a rug go dtí an ball seo é.

Ach tuigeann sé chomh tromchúiseach
Is atá an choiscéim seo, cé gur beag
Idir an charraig seo agus an charraig thall.

Tuigeann sé gur beag idir ainm is anam,
Gur mór idir friotal agus balbhacht,
Gur beag idir taobh tíre agus iontaobhas.

Tógann sé an choiscéim, coiscéim a fhágann
Lorg ar an aer. Cromann sé láithreach
Ar nótaí a bhreacadh dá leabhar athgabhála.

Toponomist

for Breandán Ó Cíobháin

He lingers for a space at Carraig Coiscéim,
Weighing the rhythm tide that surges in
And out following the weather's rubric.

He doesn't know if it is the inhabitants' voice,
The utterances of the tide, or folklore floating
Still in the air that brought him here.

But he knows well just how crucial
This footstep is, although there's little between
This rock over here and that rock over there.

He knows there is little between naming and animating,
That there is much between articulation and silence,
That there is little between landscape and inscape.

He takes the footstep, a footstep that leaves
An imprint on the air. He begins on the spot
To jot down notes for his book of repossession.

Dónal Óg

You're going, I know
Now, you'll forget how we said
We'd make our life one long holiday.
And in bed ... something
You'd only dream about here.

Last night
The dog barked, late.
Snipe jinked, cackling, towards the bog.
(No other, please God never another)
By the sheep-pen,
You said. Last night
The lambs bleated at my innocence.

My mother says she
Warned me. Wise woman,
Late, wise, beaked,
Warning woman.

Nowhere
To turn. Too desperate
For God. Men just go,
The full sorry known.
Black behind smiles. Swelling,
Spinning towards no place. God
Forgive me, I'll take the boat.

after the anonymous Irish song

Seán Ó Duibhir's Complaint

Warm dawnlight
Searched through branches
Startling dews, scattering mists,
Putting the run on dakness.
Birdsong chased the stragglers
From view. Sunlight bugled us
Awake to the hunt.
Halloo the day, the badger
And the hare! Curlew's treble
Echoed among pellets,
Counterpointed yelling,
All the glorious rírá!
And the crack we had
With the oul' one on the rod—
How we'd take a mighty revenge
For her bloody geese!
"There he goes, over the hill!
Don't worry ma'am, we'll get him
And bring you the brush!"

That was before
They cut the trees.

Now a wind
Like a long black groan
Shrivels everything.
My young lad frets
Because the hounds whimper,
Tied up for fear
They'd ramble the mean fields
Our new settlers ploughed,
Axing roots.

To think of the rutting stag
Making an appearance
Above there on the rock:
Scattering the gold of the furze
From his shoulders, flaunting
His spread antlers as if
To balance the sun until doomsday!

And they say
They'll make rich land of it.

Leave me alone for them.
I'm abroad, one way
Or another, Beyond
The sea or beyond
The law. I won't settle.

after the anonymous Irish song

In Clonmel Jail

A year tells a lot.
I never thought a year
Away with the Whiteboys,
Maiming cattle,
Would teach me the difference
Between the lurch of a hamstrung
Beast, and the jerk, tomorrow,
Of the hangman's rope.

That's a mighty jump.
At home, on the beach
Between the Iveragh hills,
The hurlers are breathless,
Turning and swinging
On the ball. That's something
To save breath for. There's
A great jump!

Even the accents jar here,
Stretched, distorted words. Listen!
The condemned man requests a hearty
Kerry accent, even in a last prayer.
I ventured a long way.
My face will soon show it:
Out in all weathers, spiked
Over Clonmel Gate.

after the anonymous Irish song

207

Marbhna Oisín

i.m. Oisín O'Mahony, naíonán

Mar gur ar éigean ar shroich tú Tír na nÓg
    Sular sciobadh arís siar thar farraige thú
Mar nár thuigis riamh draíocht na dúthaí sin
    Ná fós arís a bheith dá ceal
Mar ná rabhais riamh faoi gheasa chinn óir
    Ná aon chapall bhán faoi smacht na lámha agat
Mar nach raibh agat aon agallamh le seanóirí
    Ná seanchas peile, ná camán id lámh agat
Mar gur robáladh an taisce a shamhlaigh d'athair duit
    Agus aisling gheal do mháthar
Is id dhiaidhse atáthar, Oisín, is tá an saol ar fad
    Titithe as a riocht, mar ghaiscíoch ón diallait.

Lament for Oisín

i.m. Oisín O'Mahoney, infant

Because you had barely reached Tír na nÓg
    Before you were swept back out to sea again,
Because you never realised the magic of that place
    Nor yet again what it is to lose it,
Because you were never spellbound by golden hair
    Nor held the reins of a white horse in your hands,
Because you had never conversed with old men,
    Never talked football, nor gripped a hurley,
Because your father was robbed of the treasure he imagined,
    And your mother of her brightest dreaming,
We are forlorn, Oisín, and the whole world
    Has tumbled to the ground, like a hero from the
saddle.

Two Stories of Goats and Mountains

for Paddy Moulcore O'Sullivan

I

Coitir na Gruaige they called him, the ponytailed
Travelling man who followed his own calendar
The length and breadth of the peninsula
With his donkey and the set of uillean-pipes
That used to earn his night's bed and board,
Coaxing out whole villages with polka sets
Or the old intricacies of *Gol na mBan san Ár.*
But after he had climbed the steep slope
Of Teeromoyle, up to where the cliffs
Drop straight down into Coomasaharn,
It was his own tune that he played
To coax down the herd of goats he kept there,
A token of something best known to himself.
And they climbed down through the mist,
Gravely, like bearded elders, picking
Their steps gracefully along ledges that turned
Here and there between crags, their great horns
And yellow eyes softening into little bleats
As his drones and chanter scaled the cliffs
And he fingered his loving, familiar way
Around every last turn and grace-note
Of his own tune, the one they knew so well.

II

The other story had no music,
As I first heard it, and still
It plays jigs and reels, and tosses
Its small hooves around my mind
In unbelievable rhythms. Just imagine:
A crystal alpine sky and, in a cleft
Where a patch of frozen snow clings on,
A hiker sees a group of chamois goats
Queue to slide down one after one
On their rumps, then up straight again
Like little four-legged Pickwicks, wagging
Frozen crystals off their still tingling tails.

She swore she saw it. I imagine she did.

No Bad Blood

i.m. Paul Concannon

The grudge match between the cells is over now,
The score for once and for all settled
Between red and white (the same red and white
As the flag they draped across your coffin).
It was all against the run of the play.

God knows you were always in a rush,
Tearing through your blood-and-bandaged youth
On giddy streets and football fields or, *ó mo léar*,
Confined in your classroom, until the abrupt,
Untimely death of your father speeded you
Into adulthood and all its attendant business
Made all of the cogs of your life mesh,
Fine-tuning you towards marriage, children,
Welding, smoothing you to your true finish.
And look at you, on worthy committees,
Half-disbelieving your sense of responsibility!
And look at us, all disbelieving you, so early,
Ó mo léar, coffined in your living-room!

God knows, too, how you lubricated
Customers with *plámás*, high-octane talk
To squeeze the last mile from the gallon!
Now you've driven your own, last, hard bargain.
So there you go, for good, smiling,
Swearing, eyes thrown to heaven,
With never a drop of bad blood between
You and the wide, wide world.

Holy Mountain

for Alicia Torres

It rises from the plain without the mediation
Of foothills. From far away the pilgrims
Have seen its gullied shoulders,
The scree gilding its summit, the huts
For prayer and rest along its paths.
All of this is still as crystal clear
As it always has been. Nor is language
Now a barrier among the stalls and tents
Where the common currency of necessity
Has become a *lingua franca* among pilgrims,
Guides, penitents, beggars, stallholders and priests.
There is no fighting between those who arrive
Dusty and exhausted on the backs of animals
And those who roll smoothly to the doors
Of their appointed lodgings. Much, it seems,
Has improved, without essential change.

Tomorrow, guides and pilgrims alike will delight
In the mountain's display of flowers, and drink
Joyfully from blessed wells along the paths.
The pilgrims, however, will know nothing
Of the different tastes and textures of the wells:
Which rinses eyes the clearest, which soonest cools
The anger of the world, which best nourishes
Bud, blossom and fruit together in the mind.
The guides, when naming multicoloured flowers,
Will not be able to remember which petals
Possess the cure for which season's illnesses,
Which leaves, distilled, will make an ink

Fine enough to preserve the mountain's scriptures,
Nor which roots tap deepest into the suffering heart.

As if the mountain had laboured for centuries
Simply to delight with the clarity of its waters,
The colours of its flowers! For this the mountain
Weeps softly, persistently, throughout the night.

The Monk

In his long robes, he glides quietly
Through the streets of the Old City,
Mainly by night, when the cold
Has scattered the hawkers and buskers

And left the cobbled, gas-lit bridges
To their statues and their prostrate beggars.
The fog that rises from the river
Beads the small, wire-framed glasses

Through which he once again absorbs
The iconography of that steepled skyline
And reads the manuscript of a past
Suddenly illuminated around a corner.

The city he walks is its own reliquary,
Its winding streets the hallowed bones
Of sainted empire. He hurries home
To his mother's house, averting his eyes

From bars and cabarets. Sometimes
He pauses when a woman lights a lamp
In an upstairs room, throwing light and shadow
Across a vaulted ceiling that is new to him.

Black Dogs

for John P.

Hilarity, yes, but also the only-half-smiling
Faces and tears of the counsellors
As we followed the wheelbarrowed body
Of the addiction centre's house dog
To the hedgerowed corner of the field.
Cara. Friend. Its name resonated
As the still shining black body
Was tipped easily into the grave.

I remember how I longed for a friend,
An *anamchara*, that first evening
As we filed back to therapy, each one
Of us digging deep in the clay
Of our own thoughts, each one
Aching to bury our own black dog.

Talbot Grove, 25 April 2007

Bowl

for Theo and Paula

I was far from my own harbour, rudderless,
Taking water, no star or landmark visible
In heaving seas, or sky, or wind-rent mind.

You brought me to your house, your haven,
Caulked gaping seams, tarred thin planks,
Provisioned me to limp in safety home.

In gratitude, I bring you from my voyage
This porcelain bowl from the East, seamless,
Its fragile translucency fashioned to last.

Balance it freely in your palm, flick it
With a testing finger: it will ring true,
The note confident in the temper of its clay.

Fill it with water, and hold the pattern
Of clear-glazed pinholes to the sun: brimful,
It will spill only light, more exquisite light.